CBSE Term II 2022

Computer Applications
Class IX

- Complete Theory in Sync with Syllabus
- Case Based Questions
- Short/Long Answer Questions
- 3 Practice Papers with Explanations

Author
Dr. Garima Verma

arihant

ARIHANT PRAKASHAN (School Division Series)

ARIHANT PRAKASHAN (School Division Series)

ꖂ **Administrative & Production Offices**

Regd. Office
'Ramchhaya' 4577/15, Agarwal Road, Darya Ganj, New Delhi -110002
Tele: 011- 47630600, 43518550

ꖂ **Head Office**
Kalindi, TP Nagar, Meerut (UP) - 250002, Tel: 0121-7156203, 7156204

ꖂ **Sales & Support Offices**
Agra, Ahmedabad, Bengaluru, Bareilly, Chennai, Delhi, Guwahati, Hyderabad, Jaipur, Jhansi, Kolkata, Lucknow, Nagpur & Pune.

ꖂ **ISBN :** 978-93-25796-59-1

ꖂ **PRICE :** ₹125.00

PO No : TXT-XX-XXXXXXX-X-XX

Published by Arihant Publications (India) Ltd.

For further information about the books published by Arihant, log on to www.arihantbooks.com or e-mail at info@arihantbooks.com

Follow us on   

Contents

Watch Free Learning Videos

Subscribe **arihant**  Channel

☑ Video Solutions of CBSE Sample Papers
☑ Chapterwise Important MCQs
☑ CBSE Updates

Syllabus

CBSE Term II Class IX

No.	Units	Marks
1.	Basics of Information Technology	20
2.	Office Tools - II	5

UNIT - 1 BASICS OF INFORMATION TECHNOLOGY

- Computer Systems: characteristics of a computer, components of a computer system – CPU, memory, storage devices and I/O devices
- Memory: primary (RAM and ROM) and secondary memory
- Storage devices: hard disk, CD ROM, DVD, pen/flash drive, memory stick
- I/O devices: keyboard, mouse, monitor, printer, scanner, web camera
- Types of software: system software (operating system, device drivers), application software including mobile applications
- Computer networking: Type of networks: PAN, LAN, MAN, WAN, wired/wireless communication, Wi-Fi, Bluetooth, cloud computers (private/public)
- Multimedia: images, audio, video, animation

UNIT - 3 OFFICE TOOLS – II

Presentation Tools

- Edit and format a slide: add titles, subtitles, text, background, and watermark, headers and footers, and slide numbers.
- Insert pictures from files, create animations, add sound effects, and rehearse timings.

Spreadsheets

- Spreadsheets: concept of a worksheet and a workbook, create and save a worksheet.
- Working with a spreadsheet: enter numbers, text, date/time, series using auto fill; edit and format a worksheet including changing the colour, size, font, alignment of text; insert and delete cells, rows and columns. Enter a formula using the operators (+,-,*, /), refer to cells, and print a worksheet.
- Use simple statistical functions: SUM ( ), AVERAGE ( ), MAX ( ), MIN ( ), IF ( ) (without compound statements); embed charts of various types: line, pie, scatter, bar and area in a worksheet.

CBSE Circular

Acad - 51/2021, 05 July 2021

Exam Scheme Term I & II

केन्द्रीय माध्यमिक शिक्षा बोर्ड

(शिक्षा मंत्रालय, भारत सरकार के अधीन एक स्वायत संगठन)

CENTRAL BOARD OF SECONDARY EDUCATION

(An Autonomous Organisation under the Ministryof Education, Govt. of India)

Term I Examinations:

- At the end of the first term, the Board will organize **Term I Examination** in a flexible schedule to be conducted between November-December 2021 with a window period of 4-8 weeks for schools situated in different parts of country and abroad. Dates for conduct of examinations will be notified subsequently.
- The Question Paper will have Multiple Choice Questions (MCQ) including case-based MCQs and MCQs on assertion-reasoning type. Duration of test will be **90 minutes** and it will cover only the rationalized syllabus of **Term I only** (i.e. approx. 50% of the entire syllabus).
- Question Papers will be sent by the CBSE to schools along with marking scheme.
- The exams will be conducted under the supervision of the External Center Superintendents and Observers appointed by CBSE.
- The responses of students will be captured on OMR sheets which, after scanning may be directly uploaded at CBSE portal or alternatively may be evaluated and marks obtained will be uploaded by the school on the very same day. The final direction in this regard will be conveyed to schools by the Examination Unit of the Board.
- Marks of the **Term I** Examination will contribute to the final overall score of students.

Term II Examination/ Year-end Examination:

- At the end of the second term, the Board would organize **Term II or Year-end Examination** based on the rationalized syllabus of Term II only (i.e. approximately 50% of the entire syllabus).
- This examination would be held around **March-April 2022** at the examination centres fixed by the Board.
- The paper will be of **2 hours duration** and have questions of different formats (case-based/ situation based, open ended- short answer/ long answer type).
- In case the situation is not conducive for normal descriptive examination **a 90 minute MCQ based exam** will be conducted at the end of the Term II also.
- Marks of the Term II Examination would contribute to the final overall score.

To cover this situation, we have given both MCQs and Subjective Questions in each Chapter.

केन्द्रीय माध्यमिक शिक्षा बोर्ड

(शिक्षा मंत्रालय, भारत सरकार के अधीन एक स्वायत संगठन)

CENTRAL BOARD OF SECONDARY EDUCATION

(An Autonomous Organisation under the Ministryof Education, Govt. of India)

Assessment / Examination as per different situations

A. In case the situation of the pandemic improves and students are able to come to schools or centres for taking the exams.

Board would conduct Term I and Term II examinations at schools/centres and the theory marks will be distributed equally between the two exams.

B. In case the situation of the pandemic forces complete closure of schools during November-December 2021, but Term II exams are held at schools or centres.

Term I MCQ based examination would be done by students online/offline from home - in this case, the weightage of this exam for the final score would be reduced, and weightage of Term II exams will be increased for declaration of final result.

C. In case the situation of the pandemic forces complete closure of schools during March-April 2022, but Term I exams are held at schools or centres.

Results would be based on the performance of students on Term I MCQ based examination and internal assessments. The weightage of marks of Term I examination conducted by the Board will be increased to provide year end results of candidates.

D. In case the situation of the pandemic forces complete closure of schools and Board conducted Term I and II exams are taken by the candidates from home in the session 2021-22.

Results would be computed on the basis of the Internal Assessment/Practical/Project Work and Theory marks of Term-I and II exams taken by the candidate from home in Class X / XII subject to the moderation or other measures to ensure validity and reliability of the assessment.

In all the above cases, data analysis of marks of students will be undertaken to ensure the integrity of internal assessments and home based exams.

Dr. Joseph Emmanuel
Director (Academics)

CHAPTER 01

Computer System Organisation

In this Chapter...

- Characteristics of a Computer
- Components of a Computer
- Input Devices
- Output Devices
- Applications of a Computer

A computer is an electronic device that manipulates information or data according to the set of instructions, i.e. programs. We are surrounded by computers now-a-days. It has the ability to store, retrieve and process the data. It is used to type documents, send E-mails and browse the Internet. It is also used to handle spreadsheets, accounting, database, presentations, games and many more.

Generally, computer is the combination of hardware and software, which converts data into information. Hardware is a collection of all physical components such as scanner, keyboard, printer, monitor, CPU, floppy disk, hard disk, etc. While, software comprises the entire set of programs, procedures and routines associated with the operation of a computer system. e.g. web browsers, word processor, etc.

Computer system

Characteristics of a Computer

There are various characteristics of a computer, which are as follows

- **Accuracy** Computer operates with very high degree of accuracy and can do 100% error free calculations.

- **Speed** Computer is generally known for its speed. It can process data very fast at the rate of millions of instructions per second. Units of speed is measured in microseconds, nanoseconds and picoseconds.

- **Diligence** A computer can perform millions of tasks or calculatons with the same consistency and accuracy. It does not feel any fatigue and lack of concentration. Its memory also makes it superior to that of human beings.

- **Automaticity** It means that once the program is loaded in the memory of the computer system, the operations which are instructed by the program are performed one after the other without any human interference.

- **Versatility** Computer is highly versatile in nature. It fits into different fields of human endeavour ranging from business, education, technology, engineering, law, commerce, agriculture, medicine, sports etc. It can perform different types of tasks which are provided in a logical way to execute.

- **Large Storage Capacity** Data can be stored electronically in considerably less space which can be retrieved in a fraction of the time when needed. A limited amount of data can be stored temporarily in primary memory of computer. For permanent storage of data, secondary storage devices are used.
- **Plug and Play** Computer has the ability to automatically configure a new hardware and software components.

Components of a Computer

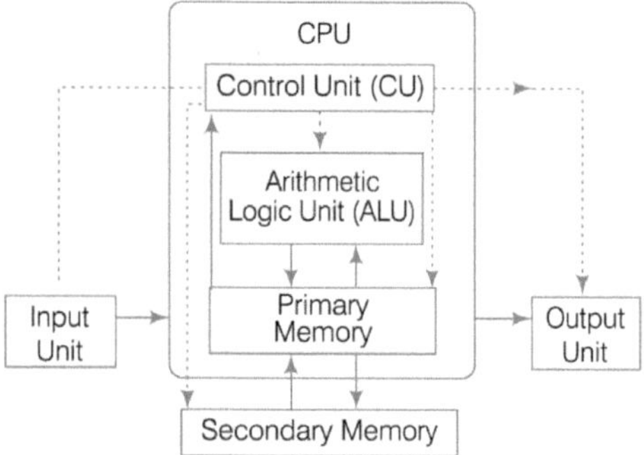

Components of a computer

Every computer system has the basic components

(i) **Input Unit** Data and instructions must enter the computer system before any computation that can be performed on the supplied data. The input unit that links the external environment with the computer system performs this task. It enters input in the form that depends upon the particular device used.

(ii) **Central Processing Unit (CPU)** It is the hardware within a computer system that carries out the instructions of a computer program to perform the basic arithmetical, logical and input/output operations of the system. CPU is also known as **brain of the computer**. The speed of CPU depends upon the type of microprocessor used and it is measured in MegaHertz (MHz).

There are two major components of the CPU, which are as follows

- **Arithmetic Logic Unit (ALU)** In computing, an ALU is a digital circuit that performs arithmetical and logical operations. It is a fundamental building block of the CPU of a computer.

  Most ALUs can perform the following operations

  - **Arithmetic operations** (addition ($+$), subtraction ($-$), multiplication ($*$) and division ($/$)).
  - **Logical operations** (AND, NOT, OR, XOR).
  - **Bit-shifting operations** (shifting or rotating a word by a specified number of bits to the left or right, with or without sign extension).
  - **Comparison operations** ($=$, $<$, $<=$, $>$, $>=$).

- **Control Unit (CU)** It coordinates the input and output devices of a computer system. It fetches the instructions which are given in the form of microprograms and directs the operation of the other units by providing timing and control signals.

  CU is the circuit that controls the flow of data through the processor and coordinates the activities of the other units within it. It acts like human nerves system, which does not process data but behaves as a central unit for other data-manipulating components. So, it is also known as nerve centre of a computer system.

(iii) **Memory Unit (MU)** This unit is responsible to store programs or data on a temporary or permanent basis. It has primary memory and secondary memory. The needed instruction for processing and any kind of intermediate results are also stored in primary memory. Another kind of memory is referred as secondary memory of a computer system. This unit is used to permanently store data.

(iv) **Output Unit** The job of an output unit is just the reverse of an input unit. It supplies information and results of computation to the outside world. Thus, it links the computer with the external environment.

Input Devices

It is a hardware device that sends data into the computer system. These devices are used to input (or enter) data and instructions into the computer system. All instructions are accepted by the CPU through electrical pulses from various kinds of input devices.

Some of the input devices are explained as follows

1. Keyboard

It is the most commonly used input device which uses an arrangement of buttons and keys. Both data and program can be entered into the computer through the keyboard. It is an essential device for interactive processing because user can easily issue commands to receive the data response immediately on the computer screen.

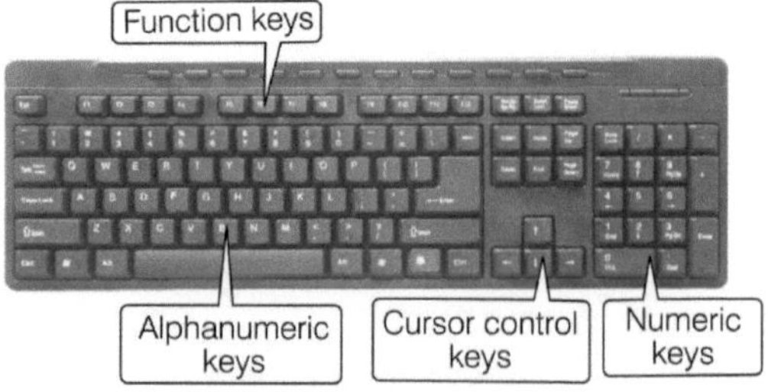

Layout of a keyboard

Types of keys on keyboard are as follows

- **Alphanumeric keys** All of the letters and numbers on the keyboard are A-Z and 0-9.
- **Punctuation keys** Such as comma (,), period (.), semicolon (;), brackets(), parentheses and so on.
- **Special keys** Such as Control key, Arrow keys, Caps lock key, Delete key, Alt key, Shift key etc.
- **Function keys** Keys labelled from F1 to F12. These keys have different meaning depends on running program.
- **Cursor Control keys** Include four directional (left or right, up or down) arrow keys that are arranged in a inverted T formation between the alphanumeric and numeric keypad.

Advantages of a Keyboard

The advantages of a keyboard are as follows

(i) Way of entering text and numbers into computer is quite simple and easy.

(ii) Available in variety of formats, such as multimedia and simple.

(iii) Keyboards have special keys that perform special functions.

Disadvantages of a Keyboard

The disadvantages of a keyboard are as follows

(i) For entering some specific type of data (e.g. pictures, diagrams, voice, video etc.), keyboard is not much useful.

(ii) Very slow while selecting menu options or various objects displayed on the screen.

(iii) Sometimes, it is needed to use number of keys or combination of specific keys to perform some task.

2. Mouse

It is a pointing device that allows to control the movement of a pointer (also known as **mouse pointer**) on screen. It performs various functions by detecting two-dimensional motion relatively to its supporting surface. It can be of different types like wired mouse, wireless mouse, optical mouse, mechanical mouse etc. Generally, it has two buttons, i.e. a **right button** and a **left button**. It also includes a **scroll wheel** between the buttons to scroll up and down the application window and their contents also.

Wired mouse

Wireless mouse

Different types of mouse are as follows

- **Mechanical mouse** In this type of mouse, movement of a cursor on the screen is relative to the movement of the ball available at the bottom of the mouse.
- **Optical mouse** It uses a Light Emitting Diode (LED) and photodiodes to detect movement.
- **Laser mouse** It uses Infrared Laser Diode instead of a normal LED.
- **Wireless mouse** It communicates with the computer *via* radio waves (often using bluetooth hardware and software), so that a cord is not needed (but such mouse needs internal batteries).

Note A pointing device is a human interface device that allows the user to move the cursor to a computer.

Advantages of a Mouse

The advantages of a mouse are as follows

(i) Ideal for pointing objects/options.

(ii) Most familiar and easy to use.

(iii) Works very well for navigating a Graphical User Interface (GUI).

Disadvantages of a Mouse

The disadvantages of a mouse are as follows

(i) Need a flat space close to computer.

(ii) Wired mouses cannot easily be used with a laptop, notebook or palmtop computers.

3. Scanner

It is a device that allows a user to take an image or a text and convert it into a digital file, allowing the computer to read or display the scanned object. Scanner can be used for storing the documents in their original form that can be modified and manipulated later on.

Scanner

Scanner comes in a variety of size from hand-held models to desktop models, which are as follows

- **Hand-held scanners** They are very small which can be held in a hand. These are less expensive and less wide. Hence, in order to scan a single page image, multiple passes are required. But, their handiness is a major advantage of it.
- **Flatbed scanners** They are large and more expensive scanners that create higher quality of images. These scanners have a flat surface on which the printed image to be scanned is placed (similar to the way a page is placed on a photocopier). They can scan a page in a single pass.

- **Drum scanners** They are medium size scanners with a rolling drum. The sheet is fed through the scanners, so that the drum rolls over the entire sheet to be scanned (just as the sheets are fed in a fax machine).

Advantages of a Scanner

The advantages of a scanner are as follows
  (i) Easy to use and install.
  (ii) Gives the copy of a document in digital format.
  (iii) Works like a photocopy machine.

Disadvantages of a Scanner

The disadvantages of a scanner are as follows
  (i) Quality of digital image depends on the quality of original image.
  (ii) Easily broken if get hit.
  (iii) Too big to carry around.

4. Web Camera (Webcam)

It is a digital camera attached to computers and can be used for video conferencing or online chatting etc. It is also able to capture full motion videos. It is connected to a computer that allows the user to view either a still picture or a motion video of a user or other object. Now-a-days, it is embedded into the display with laptops or connected *via* USB or firewire port or Wi-Fi to the computer system. After connecting webcam to a computer, you need to install required software or drivers.

A Webcam attached with computer

Webcam

Advantages of a Web Camera

The advantages of a web camera are as follows
  (i) Enables a user to interact with people across long distances.
  (ii) Both sound and video are used, making the communication better.
  (iii) Users can use the webcam to save videos and can watch them later or send to others.

Disadvantages of a Web Camera

The disadvantages of a web camera are as follows
  (i) Discourages people to interact face-to-face.
  (ii) Can be used to film inappropriate/illegal videos.
  (iii) Hackers can enable webcams even when, the owner is not aware.

Output Devices

It is a part of computer hardware equipment, used to communicate the results of data processing which are carried out by information processing system (such as a computer), to the outside world. It carries the results of various operations performed by the user. Some of the devices, which are used to display the processed result or output are as follows

1. Monitor

A monitor (called a **Visual Display Unit**-VDU) is an electronic visual device used to display the output. The rectangular area of the monitor, its refresh rate and dot pitch, all directly affect the resolution of the display.

> **Resolution**
> It refers to the clarity of screen and measured by the number of individual tiny colored dots (known as **pixels**), scattered on the screen. Resolution indicates the number of dots per inch (dpi).

Types of Monitor

The popular types of monitor are as follows
  (i) **CRT** (Cathode Ray Tube) It works in the same way as a television. It contains an electron gun at the back of the glass tube. This gun fires electrons in a group of phosphor dots, which is coated inside the screen. When electrons strike the phosphor dots, they glow to give the colors.

CRT monitor

  (ii) **LCD** (Liquid Crystal Display) These screens are used in laptops and notebook sized PCs. A special type of liquid is sandwiched between two plates. It is a thin, flat and light weight screen made up of any number of colors or monochrome pixels arranged in front of a light source.

LCD monitor

  (iii) **LED** (Liquid/Light Emitting Diode) It is an electronic device that emits light when electrical current is passed through it. It usually produces red light, but now-a-days LEDs can produce RGB (Red, Green and Blue) lights and white light also.

LED monitor

(iv) **3-D Monitor** It is a television that conveys depth perception to the viewer. It describes an image that provides the perception of length. When 3-D images are made interactive, user feels involved with the scene and this experience is called **virtual reality**.

3-D monitor

Advantages of a Monitor

The advantages of a monitor are as follows

(i) Displays both text and graphic images.

(ii) It is available in various sizes like 8", 12", 14", 15", 17", 19" and 21".

(iii) Various kinds of monitors are available in black and white or colored.

Disadvantages of a Monitor

The disadvantages of a monitor are as follows

(i) Only limited amount of information can be displayed at a time.

(ii) CRT screens are made up of glass and can be fragile.

(iii) CRT monitor has low refreshing ability which is known as **flickering effect**.

2. Printer

It is an output device, which produces a hard copy of documents that are stored in an electronic form on physical print media such as paper or transparencies. So, printers are the primary output devices used to prepare permanent documents. The speed of a printer is normally rated either by Pages Per Minute (PPM) or by Characters Per Second (CPS). The quality of the image is determined by the Dots Per Inch (DPI).

Types of Printer

It can be classified into two broad categories, which are as follows

(i) Impact Printers

These rely on a forcible impact to transfer ink to the print media, similar to the action of a typewriter. There is a mechanical contact between the paper and the print head.

The main types of impact printers are as follows

(a) **Line printer** It is impact shaped character printer, which are capable of printing an entire line at once instead of one or more characters at a time. Printing quality of line printer is not high.

Line printer

(b) **Drum printer** It is printer technology that is used to form character images around a cylindrical drum as its printing mechanism. When the desired character for the selected position rotated around the hammer line, the hammer hit the paper from behind and pushed it into the ribbon and onto the character.

Drum printer

(c) **Daisy wheel printer** It can print one character at a time. In daisy wheel printer, round disk extends a portion of the wheel making contact with ink ribbon that makes contact with paper for creating the character. This procedure is repeated for each key, when it is pressed. These printers are fitted with unchangeable print heads called **daisy wheels**. To print each character, the wheel is rotated and the appropriate stroke struck against an ink ribbon. It cannot produce high quality print graphics. The speed of daisy wheel printer is about 100 cps.

(d) **Dot-matrix printer** The term dot-matrix refers to the process of placing dots to form an image. It uses print heads to shoot ink or strike an ink ribbon to place hundreds to thousands of little dots to form text or images. It prints one character at a time. The speed of dot-matrix printer lies between 100 to 600 cps. These printers are slow and noisy that are not commonly used for personal computers. They can print multi-layer forms. It can print special characters and graphic and does not have fixed character fonts.

Advantages of an Impact Printer

The advantages of an impact printer are as follows
  (i) Installation cost is low.
  (ii) They are robust and can be used in harsh conditions.
  (iii) It creates the characters by striking on the paper.

Disadvantages of an Impact Printer

The disadvantages of an impact printer are as follows
  (i) Print quality is too poor to produce documents.
  (ii) Printing speed is less than 600 characters per minute.
  (iii) Cannot produce color copies.

(ii) Non-impact Printers

These printers much quieter than impact printers as their printing heads do not strike on the paper. Most of non-impact printers produce dot-matrix patterns. There is no mechanical contact between the paper and the print head. These printers are comparatively faster and produce high quality output. They can be used for printing text and graphics both in black and white and colored.

The main types of non-impact printers are as follows
  (a) **Electromagnetic printer** Electrographic or electro-photographic printers are very fast printers, which fall under the category of page printers. They can produce documents at a speed of over 20,000 lines per minute, i.e. more than 250 pages per minute. The electrographic technology has developed from the paper copier technology.
  (b) **Thermal printer** These printer paper tends to darken over time due to exposure of sunlight or heat. The quality of produced print is poor. It is widely used in battery powered equipment such as portable calculators.
  (c) **Electrostatic printer** These printers are generally used for large format printing and favoured by large printing shops because of their ability to print fast and making low cost.
  (d) **Laser printer** In this printer, the method of printing is based on principle of electro-photography and use a beam of laser light as a photocopy machine. It is the most expensive printer.

Laser printer

The powdered ink (i.e. toner) is transferred to paper in the form of text/image pattern and then fixed by heat or pressure. When used to print bulk of papers, the laser printer produces the cheapest cost per printout. It has very high resolution from 600-1200 dpi (dots per inch) but, cost of maintenance and repairing is high due to complex equipment set inside the printer. It occupies a lot of space and emits dust particles that can cause respiratory diseases.

  (e) **Inkjet printer** It fires extremely small droplets of ink onto the paper to create impression of text or image. The print-head of inkjet printers, known as print cartridge, contains tiny nozzles (50 or more) through which different colored inks can be sprayed onto the paper to form the characters or graphic images.

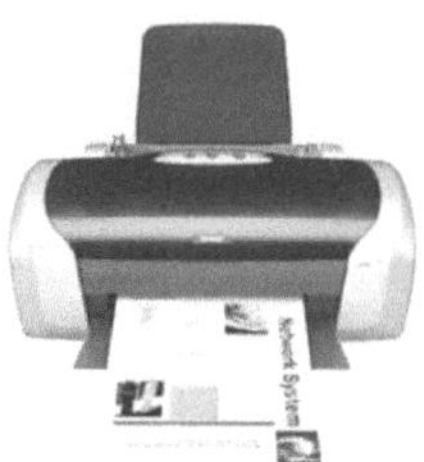
Inkjet printer

Color inkjet printers provide an inexpensive way to print fully colored documents. It has good resolution usually 300-600 dpi and capable of printing in vivid colors but, color printing can take 25-30 seconds for each page.

Inkjet printer is fast as compared to a dot-matrix printer but, slow as compared to a laser printer.

Advantages of a Non-impact Printer

The advantages of a non-impact printer are as follows
  (i) Much lower ink cost over time.
  (ii) Less maintenance.
  (iii) Much more reliable.
  (iv) Better for multi-use.

Disadvantages of a Non-impact Printer

The disadvantages of a non-impact printer are as follows
  (i) Cannot print multipart forms.
  (ii) More costly to replace cartridges for a laser printer.
  (iii) Harder to use with old PC's.

Applications of a Computer

Now-a-days, computer has been employed in almost all the aspects of professional and personal life of human beings. Some of the areas where computers are being used are as follows
  (i) **Education** Computer has proved to be an excellent teacher. Educational institutes are using computers in many ways like tele-education, virtual classroom, online classes etc.

(ii) **Science** Scientists have been long users of computer. A new adventure among scientists is the idea of a collaboratory (Internet based collaborative laboratory) in which researchers from all over the world can work together easily even at a distance.

(iii) **Industry** Computer is used to control manufacturing systems and continuous running of the machinery. Parameters like temperature, pressure, volume are monitored and controlled by computers. Robotics developed with the help of computers which play a very crucial role.

(iv) **Recreation and Entertainment** Computers in recreation and entertainment are the ones that are divided into various categories, i.e. social, communication, sports, music and games. Thus, people look forward to the entertainment for recreation, so that they can reduce their stress and strains of their complex machined like schedules.

(v) **Government** Various departments of the government use computers for their planning, controlling and law enforcement activities. e.g. budgets, weather forecasting, income tax department etc.

(vi) **Health** Computer plays a very crucial role in this area. Activities like scanning, X-ray, tele-medicine, patient monitoring, patient records and diagnosis etc., are performed with the help of computers.

(vii) **Multimedia** It is the field concerned with the computer controlled integration of text, graphics, drawings, animation, audio and any other media, where each type of information can be represented, stored, transmitted and processed digitally.

(viii) **Banking** Computers are used in banks to keep the records of customer's accounts. It also provides online accounting facility which includes current balances, deposits, overdrafts, interest charges etc.

(ix) **Military Personnel** Computers are used for the crucial tasks like determining the weather, computing the trajectories of missiles, smart weapons etc.

(x) **Business** Using a wide range of business software, a company's marketing division can produce sales forecasts and devising new strategies.

(xi) **E-Commerce** Traditionally, commerce is seen as the exchange or buying and selling of goods and services, which involves exchange of money and sometimes transportation of goods. Electronic commerce (E-Commerce) that takes place between businesses is referred to as **Business-to-Business** or **B2B**.

Chapter Practice

Objective Questions

• Multiple Choice Questions

1. A computer is free from tiredness, monotony, etc., reflects which characteristic?
  (a) High speed   (b) Versatile
  (c) Accuracy   (d) Diligence

Ans. (*d*) Diligence is an important feature of a computer. Unlike human beings, a computer is free from monotony, tiredness and lack of concentration etc. It can do work for hours without creating any errors.

2. Which part of computer responsible for all numerical and logical calculations?
  (a) CPU   (b) CU
  (c) MU   (d) ALU

Ans. (*d*) ALU stands for Arithmetic Logic Unit, which is responsible to perform all kind of numerical and logical operations.

3. Control Unit (CU) is called the .... of a computer system.
  (a) heart
  (b) nerve centre
  (c) primary memory
  (d) All of the above

Ans. (*b*) Control unit is called a brain or nerve centre of the computer because it handles all the signals communication between all units of a computer.

4. A computer now-a-days essentially used as a
  (a) network
  (b) data processor
  (c) communication device
  (d) calculator

Ans. (*b*) Computer is an electronic device that converts data into information after processing them, therefore called as data processor.

5. Hardware is a collection of .... components.
  (a) team   (b) program
  (c) instructions   (d) physical

Ans. (*d*) The computer consists with two things- hardware and software. The hardware is a collection of all physical components of the computer such as keyboard, CPU, etc.

6. Software is a collection of
  (a) instructions   (b) sets
  (c) programs   (d) flowcharts

Ans. (*c*) Software is a part of the computer. It is actually a collection of different types of programs.

7. Which of the following does not represent an I/O device?
  (a) Speaker (b) Plotter   (c) Joystick   (d) CU

Ans. (*d*) CU does not represent on I/O device. CU (Control Unit) is the part of the Computer's Central Processing Unit (CPU), which directs the operation of the processor. Speaker and polotter are output devices while joystick is an input device.

8. Scanner is a device that allows a user to convert an image into a .... form of file.
  (a) decimal   (b) text
  (c) digital   (d) Any format

Ans. (*c*) Scanner is an input device that allows a user to scan any image and convert it into a digital form of file.

9. .... is a medium size scanner which has rolling drum to scan your documents.
  (a) Drum   (b) Hand-held
  (c) Flatbed   (d) Roller

Ans. (*a*) There are various type of scanners. Drum scanner are medium size scanners with a rolling drum. The sheet is fed through the scanners, so that the drum rolls over the entire sheet to be scanned (just as the sheets are fed in a fax machine).

10. The speed of CPU is measured in
  (a) Hertz   (b) MegaHertz
  (c) GigaHertz   (d) TeraHertz

Ans. (b) The speed of CPU depends upon the type of microprocessor used and it is measured in MegaHertz (MHz).

11. Dot-matrix is a type of
(a) line printer
(b) disk printer
(c) character printer
(d) bus printer

Ans. (c) Dot-matrix printer is a type of printer that produces characters and graphics on a piece of paper without striking. It prints by hammering a set of metal pin or character set.

12. Which input device is used to make a digital copy of a photograph?
(a) Graphics tablet   (b) Scanner
(c) MICR   (d) OMR

Ans. (b) The scanner is an input device. The main purpose of scanner is to scan any image or photo available on a paper, and convert it into a digital form of file.

13. Ctrl, Alt, Caps Lock etc, are
(a) cursor keys
(b) special keys
(c) punctuation keys
(d) functions keys

Ans. (b) Ctrl, Alt, Shift, Caps Lock, Delete etc, are all special keys.

14. The printed information on the paper is called
(a) hardware
(b) hardcopy
(c) software
(d) printer

Ans. (b) Whenever output displays on the monitor then output is called as softcopy which cannot be touched. But if we take the print of output on a paper it is called as hardcopy.

15. The speed of laser printer is rated by
(a) CCP   (b) PPM
(c) CMP   (d) PMP

Ans. (b) The laser printer in a non-impact page printer. The speed can be measure as Page Per Minute (PPM).

16. .... indicates the numbers of dots per inches.
(a) Speed   (b) Print
(c) Resolution   (d) Display

Ans. (c) Resolution refers to the clarity of screen and measures by the number of individual tiny colored dots, known as pixels. Resolution indicates the number of dots per inch (dpi).

• Case Based MCQs

Direction *Read the case and answer the following questions.*

17. A computer is an electronic device that process data and converts into the information according to the set of instructions. This set of instructions are called as programs. Computer main advantages are

- It has the ability to store, retrieve and process the data.
- It is used by companies now-a-days to make documents by typing using text editors, one can send and receive E-mails and browse the Internet.

In general, computer is the combination of hardware and software. Hardware is a collection of all physical components such as scanner, keyboard, printer, monitor, CPU, etc. While, software comprises the entire set of programs, procedures, and routines associated with the operation of a computer system. There are various characteristics of computers, such as accuracy, diligence, speed, automaticity, etc. The CPU is called as a brain of the computer. It consists with three main components – ALU, MU and CU.

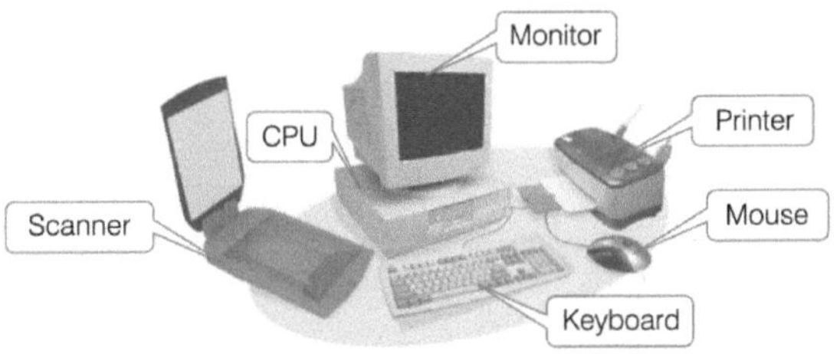

(i) Computer has an ability to
(a) store data
(b) process data
(c) retrieve data
(d) All of the above

(ii) Computer is a combination of hardware and
....
(a) software   (b) instructions
(c) flowcharts   (d) keyboard

(iii) Which is not a characteristic of a computer?
(a) Accuracy   (b) Automaticity
(c) Human like brain   (d) Speed

(iv) The .... is called as a brain of the computer.
(a) ALU   (b) input
(c) CPU   (d) output

(v) Computer main task is to convert .... into
....
(a) information, data
(b) data, information
(c) data, process
(d) process, data

Ans. (i) (*d*) Computer main advantages are – it has the ability to store, retrieve and process the data.

(ii) (*a*) Computer is the combination of hardware and software. Software comprises the entire set of programs, procedures and routines associated with the operation of a computer system.

(iii) (*c*) There are various characteristics of computers, such as accuracy, diligence, speed, automaticity, etc. Hence, human like brain is not a characteristic of a computer.

(iv) (*c*) The CPU is called as a brain of the computer. It consists with three main components – ALU, MU and CU.

(v) (*b*) Computer is the combination of hardware and software, which converts data into information.

18. Printer is an output device, it is used to produce a hard copy of documents that are stored in an electronic form on physical print media such as paper or transparencies. Printers are also used as a primary output devices and used to prepare permanent documents called as hard copy. The speed of a printer is normally measure either by Pages Per Minute (PPM) or by Characters Per Second (CPS). The quality of the print image is determined by the Dots Per Inch (DPI). There are two types of printers–impact and non-impact. The impact printers rely on a forceful impact to transfer ink to the print media, similar to the action of a typewriter using a hammer. There is a mechanical contact between the paper and the print head.

Dot matrix-printer comes under the category of impact printers. It is also consider as character printer. The main advantage of impact printer is cost and robustness. The non-impact printers much quieter than impact printers as their printing heads do not strike on the paper. There is no mechanical contact between the paper and the print head. The main advantage of non-impact printer is high quality output.

(i) The electronic form on physical print media is called as
(a) paper
(b) hard copy
(c) soft copy
(d) digital copy

(ii) The speed of a printer can be rated as .... which prints the output character-by-character.
(a) DPI   (b) PPM   (c) CPS   (d) PPS

(iii) The most common character impact printer is .... printer.
(a) laser
(b) dot-matrix
(c) inkjet
(d) drum

(iv) Impact printer main advantage is ...., while non-impact printer is ....
(a) cost, quality
(b) robust, cost
(c) cost, robust
(d) quality, cost

(v) .... is a primary output device which can be used with computer to take hard copy.
(a) Monitor
(b) Printer
(c) Scanner
(d) Plotter

Ans. (i) (*b*) Printer is an output device which is also called is physical print media device. It is used to produces a hard copy of documents that are stored in an electronic form on physical print media such as paper or transparencies.

(ii) (*c*) The speed of a printer is normally measure either by Pages Per Minute (PPM) if a printer prints one page at a time or by Characters Per Second (CPS) if a printer prints one character at a time.

(iii) (*b*) Dot-matrix printer comes under the category of impact printers.

(iv) (*a*) The main advantage of impact printer is cost and robustness. The non-impact printers much quieter than impact printers as their printing heads do not strike on the paper. There is no mechanical contact between the paper and the print head. The main advantage of non-impact printer is high quality output.

(v) (*b*) Printer is the primary output device, which is used to prepare permanent document called as hard copy.

PART 2
Subjective Questions

• Short Answer Type Questions

1. Distinguish between input unit and output unit.

Ans. The differences between input unit and output unit are as follows

Input Unit	Output Unit
It accepts the data and instructions from outside.	It accepts the result which produced by the computer.
It converts the accepted instructions and data in computer acceptable form.	It converts the results, which are in a coded form to human readable form.
It supplies the instructions and data to the computer system for further processing.	It supplies the converted results to the user.

2. Explain the diligence and versatile properties of the computer.

Ans. Diligence Computers can work for many hours continuously without taking any rest and without decreasing its speed, accuracy and efficiency. It is free from tiredness, lack of concentration, fatigue, etc.

Versatile Computer is a versatile machine, which can do varieties of task such as simple calculation to a complex and logical operation. It is used in various fields for various purposes.

3. Draw the block diagram of the computer.

Ans.

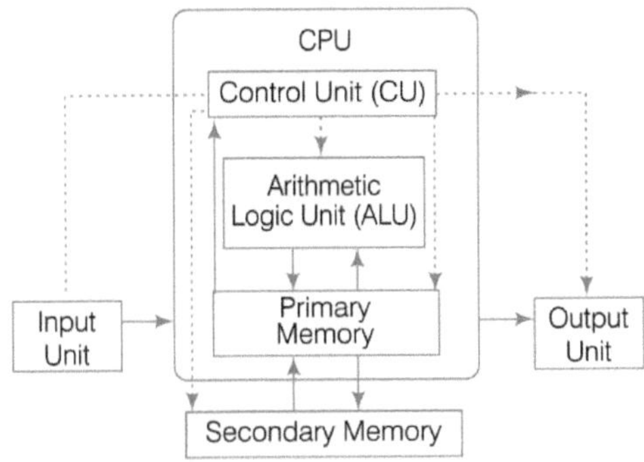

4. List some operations performed by ALU.

Ans. ALUs can perform the following operations

(i) **Arithmetic operations** (addition ($+$), subtraction ($-$), multiplication ($*$) and division ($/$)).

(ii) **Logical operations** (AND, NOT, OR, XOR).

(iii) **Bit-shifting operations** (shifting or rotating a word by a specified number of bits to the left or right, with or without sign extension).

(iv) **Comparison operations** ($=$, $<$, $<=$, $>$, $>=$).

5. Draw a neat diagram to show the parts of CPU.

Ans.

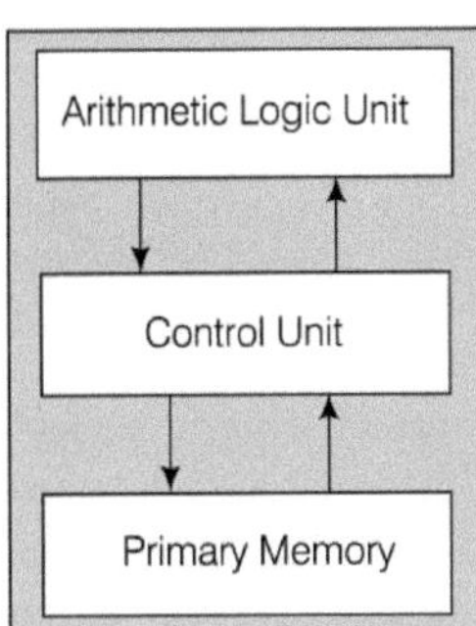

6. Explain, why control unit is called as nerve system?

Ans. Control Unit (CU) is responsible to make coordination between the input and output devices of a computer system. It takes the instructions which are given in the form of a microprograms and give signal to the other units for performing operations. The signals generated by CU are called as timing and control signals. CU controls the flow of data through the processor and coordinates the activities of the other units within it. It acts like human nerves system, which does not process data but behaves as a central unit for other data-manipulating components. Therefore, it is also known as nerve centre of a computer system.

7. Describe any two applications of computers.

Ans. Two main applications of computers are as follows

(i) **Education** Computer has proved to be an excellent teacher. Educational institutes are using computers in many ways like tele-education, virtual classroom, online classes, etc.

(ii) **Science** Scientists have been long users of computer. A new adventure among scientists is the idea of a collaboratory (Internet based collaborative laboratory) in which researchers from all over the world can work together easily even at a distance.

8. The usefulness of computers has now become a part of humanity. You cannot imagine life without them.

(i) Do computers have weaknesses also? If yes, then give some examples.

(ii) Give some uses of computer in daily life.

Ans. (i) Yes, computers have weaknesses. Some weaknesses of computers are lack of decision-making power, zero IQ and no heuristics.

(ii) Some uses of computer in daily life are listen to songs, send E-mail, watching movies, etc.

9. A computer consists with hardware and software. Hardware represents the physical components while software are the collection of programs. Instruction is the smallest unit of a program. CPU is main part of any computer also called as brain of a computer. CPU consists with Arithmetic Logic Unit (ALU), Memory unit (MU) and Control Unit (CU). The data is taken by the input unit, then feed into CPU. The memory unit stores the data for further processing. But MU can retain data till it is required or computer is on. The data will be lost if the power turned OFF. All the mathematical calculations are performed by the ALU on data and CU is called as nerve system of the computer. It generates different type of signals to control all the functioning of the computer. When the data is processed the result can be displayed on the output unit.

(i) Which part of computer is called as brain?

(ii) What is the purpose of memory unit and what kind of data retention capacity it has?

Ans. (i) The CPU is a main part of any computer, which consists with ALU, MU and CU. All the activities related to processing is done and controlled by the CPU. Due to all specified reasons, CPU is also called as brain of a computer.

(ii) The Memory Unit (MU) in computer resides as a part of CPU. The main purpose of MU is to hold data or instructions till the processing is not completed. MU can retain data till it is required or computer is On. The data will be lost if the power turned OFF.

10. Explain LCD. Write the features of an LCD monitor.

Ans. LCD stands for Liquid Crystal Display. These screens are used in notebooks and laptops sized PCs. A special type of liquid is sandwiched between two plates. It is thin, flat and light weight screen made up of any number of colors.

Some of the major features of LCD monitors are as follows

(i) Reduced radiation

(ii) Light weight

(iii) Less eyestrain

11. Explain the qualities of non-impact printers.

Ans. Non-impact printers much quieter than impact printers as their printing heads do not strike on the paper. Most of non-impact printers produce dot-matrix patterns.

There is no mechanical contact between the paper and the print head. These printers are comparatively faster and produce high quality output. They can be used for printing text and graphics both in black and white and colored.

The main types of non-impact printers are as follows

(i) Electromagnetic printer

(ii) Thermal printer

(iii) Electrostatic printer

(iv) Laser printer

(v) Inkjet printer

12. Which technology is used in laser printers for printing hard copy?

Ans. Laser printers are based on photocopy technology to print. They use a laser beam and dry powder ink to produce a high quality dot-matrix pattern. They can print graphic images too. They are ideally used when good quality and large scale printing is required.

13. Differentiate between impact and non-impact printers.

Ans. Differences between impact and non-impact printers are as follows

Impact Printer	Non-impact Printer
Produces characters and graphics on a piece of paper by striking.	A type of printer that produces characters and graphics on a piece of paper without striking.
It prints by hammering a set of metal pin.	It prints by disposing ink in any form.
Produce noise.	Works silently.
e.g. Dot-matrix	e.g. Inkjet

14. What are the advantages and disadvantages of impact printer.

Ans. The advantages of an impact printer are as follows

(i) Installation cost is low.

(ii) They are robust and can be used in harsh conditions.

(iii) It creates the characters by striking on the paper.

The disadvantages of an impact printer are as follows

(i) Print quality is too poor to produce documents.

(ii) Printing speed is less than 600 characters per minute.

(iii) Cannot produce color copies.

15. Which device can be used as an output device for generating the visual display output of results?

Ans. A monitor (called a Visual Display Unit-VDU) is an electronic visual device used to display the output. The rectangular area of the monitor, its refresh rate and dot pitch, all directly affect the resolution of the display. There are various type of monitors – CRT, LED, LCD, etc.

16. Differentiate between LED and LCD monitors of a computer.

Ans. Differences between LED and LCD monitors of a computer are as follows

LED	LCD
It is called as Light Emitting Diode monitor.	It is called as Liquid Crystal Display monitor.
It has no backlight.	Cold cathode fluorescent lamp provides backlight.
Resolution is high.	Resolution is low.

17. Name an input device which can be used for the video conferencing or online chatting. Explain it.

Ans. Webcam is a device also called as digital camera attached to computers and can be used for video conferencing or online chatting etc. It is also able to capture full motion videos. It is connected to a computer that allows the user to view either a still picture or a motion video of a user or other object. Now-a-days, it is embedded into the display with laptops or connected *via* USB or firewire port or Wi-Fi to the computer system. After connecting webcam to a computer, you need to install required software or drivers.

18. What do you mean by a **pointing device**? Name any one device which can be used as an input device with computer.

Ans. A device which uses a pointer to point items on the screen and also used to execute various commands. Mouse is a most popular input device, which comes under the category of pointing devices. It works by using a pointer movement displayed on the monitor.

19. Which device is called default input device with computer?

Ans. Keyboard is referred as a default input device. It is the most commonly used input device which uses an arrangement of buttons and keys. Both data and program can be entered into the computer through the keyboard. It is an essential device for interactive processing because user can easily issue commands to receive the data response immediately on the computer screen.

20. What are most popular categories of the keys available on a keyboard?

Ans. There are various types of keys available on keyboard

(i) **Alphanumeric keys** All of the letters and numbers on the keyboard are A-Z and 0-9.

(ii) **Punctuation keys** These keys are also called as separators, such as comma (,), period (.), semicolon (;), brackets (), parentheses and so on.

(iii) **Special keys** Control key, Arrow keys , Caps lock key, Delete key, Alt key, Shift key etc.

(iv) **Function keys** Keys labelled from F1 to F12. These keys have different meaning depends on running program.

(v) **Cursor Control keys** There are four directional (left or right, up or down) arrow keys found on the keyboard.

• Long Answer Type Questions

21. What are the characteristics of a computer?

Ans. There are various characteristics of a computer are as follows

(i) **Accuracy** Computer operates with very high degree of accuracy and can do 100% error free calculations. It does not get exhausted to the extent of making mistakes.

(ii) **Speed** Computer is generally known for its speed. It can process data very fast at the rate of millions of instructions per second. Units of speed is measured in microseconds, nanoseconds and picoseconds.

(iii) **Diligence** Unlike human beings, a computer is free from monotony, tiredness, lack of concentration etc. and can do work for hours without creating any errors.

(iv) **Automaticity** It means that once the program is loaded in the memory of the computer system, the operations which are instructed by the program are performed one after the other without any human interference.

(v) **Versatility** Computer is highly versatile in nature. It fits into different fields of human endeavour ranging from business, education, technology, engineering, law, commerce, agriculture, medicine, sports etc. It can perform different types of tasks which are provided in a logical way to execute.

(vi) **Large Storage Capacity** Data can be stored electronically in considerably less space which can be retrieved in a fraction of the time when needed. A limited amount of data can be stored temporarily in primary memory of computer. For permanent storage of data, secondary storage devices are used.

(vii) **Plug and Play** Computer has the ability to automatically configure a new hardware and software component.

22. What are the functional units of a computer?

Ans. The functional units of a computer are as follows

(i) **Input Unit** Computer takes data from input devices.

(ii) **CPU (Central Processing Unit)** It is the brain of the computer, where most of the calculations takes place. It consists of

- **ALU (Arithmetic Logic Unit)** It performs arithmetical and logical operations.

- **CU (Control Unit)** It extracts instructions from memory, decodes and executes them.

(iii) **Memory Unit** This unit is responsible to store programs or data on a temporary or permanent basis. It has primary memory and secondary memory.

(iv) **Output Unit** Gives out results or data through output devices.

23. Describe the different types of scanners.

Ans. Scanner is a device that allows a user to take an image or a text and convert it into a digital file. It also allows the computer to read or display the scanned object.
The scanner can be used for storing the documents in their original form that can be modified and manipulated later on.
Scanner can be categorised as per the variety of size from hand-held models to desktop models, which are as follows

(i) **Hand-held scanners** They are very small which can be easily held in a hand. Main advantage is quite less in cost and less wide. Hence, in order to scan a single page image, multiple passes are required. But, their handiness or extreme portability is a major advantage of it.

(ii) **Flatbed scanners** This type of scanners are large in size and more expensive scanners. These are used to create higher quality of images. These scanners have a flat surface on which the printed image to be scanned is placed (similar to the way a page is placed on a photocopier). They can scan a page in a single pass. Speed is comparatively high.

(iii) **Drum scanners** These are medium size scanners with a rolling drum inside it. The sheet is fed through the scanners so that the drum rolls over the entire sheet to be scanned.

24. Write two categories of printers. Which type of printers are more speedy and quieter?

Ans. The printers can be classified into two categories, which are as follows

(i) **Impact printers** In these types of printers, there is a mechanical contact between the paper and the print head. These can further be classified as line printers (which can print a line at a time) and daisy wheel printers (which can print a character at a time).

(ii) **Non-impact printers** In these types of printers, there is no mechanical contact between the paper and the printer head.

The printing takes place with some electromagnetic thermal or laser techniques. The non-impact printers are more speedy and quieter than impact printers.

25. Explain monitor as an output device. Explain any two types of monitor used now-a-days.

Ans. A monitor or a Visual Display Unit (VDU) is an electronic visual device used to display the output in the form of a digital form called as soft copy. Monitor or Visual Display Unit (VDU) is an input/output device which is used to display the output in digital form, called as soft copy. There are two varieties of monitor available now-a-days

(i) **LCD** (Liquid Crystal Display) These screens are used in laptops and notebook sized PCs. A special type of liquid is sandwiched between two plates. It is a thin, flat and light weight screen made up of any number of colors or monochrome pixels arranged in front of a light source.

(ii) **LED** (Liquid/Light Emitting Diode) It is an electronic device that emits light when electrical current is passed through it. It usually produces red light, but now-a-days LEDs can produce RGB (Red, Green and Blue) light and white light also.

26. Sakshi is preparing a lecture on output device like monitor. Discuss (i) advantages of 'monitor' and (ii) disadvantages of 'monitor' also.

Ans. (i) The advantages of monitor are as follows

(a) Relatively cheap and reliable.

(b) Can display text and graphics in a wide range of colors.

(ii) The disadvantages of monitor are as follows

(a) No permanent copy to keep the results as it will disappear when the computer is switched OFF.

(b) Unsuitable for users with visual problems.

Chapter Test

Multiple Choice Questions

1. .... is an electronic device that manipulates information or data according to the set of instructions called program.
   (a) Computer   (b) CPU   (c) ALU   (d) None of these

2. The speed of CPU depends upon the type of microprocessor used and it is measured in
   (a) GHZ   (b) MHZ   (c) Both (a) and (b)   (d) None of these

3. Computer can perform various functions, choose which is a correct function?
   (a) Store data   (b) Process data   (c) Display data   (d) All of these

4. The .... file can be created from image using scanner.
   (a) decimal   (b) text
   (c) digital   (d) Any format

5. Drum scanner is a medium size scanner which has .... to scan documents.
   (a) rolling drum   (b) hand-held   (c) flatbed   (d) roller

6. A printer which can be called as a character printer.
   (a) Drum printer   (b) Disk printer
   (c) Dot-matrix printer   (d) Laser printer

Short Answer Type Questions

7. Write short note on computer systems.

8. Rama, a class IX student, is learning computers. Yesterday her teacher taught a chapter about input devices and gave an assignment. Help him do so.
   (i) Which of the following statements are true about input devices?
      (a) Input device is any software device.
      (b) Input device allows user to interact with computer.
      (c) Keyboard is an input device.
      (d) Input devices are not visible.
   (ii) Name few input devices.

9. Identify input/output devices from the clues given below:
   (i) Transfers typed or handwritten texts, graphs, diagrams and photographs into a digital format.
   (ii) Produces images on paper such as numbers, alphabets and graphics.
   (iii) Can be used for video conferencing or online chatting.

10. Mohan have been given certain devices to complete an assignment. Given devices are – Keyboard, Printer, Scanner and Pen drive. Identify, which kind of task Mohan can perform from these devices?

Long Answer Type Questions

11. Vishnu is a student of class IX. Teacher asked him to give the name of input and output devices as per the following requirements. Help him to identify devices.
    (i) Device should be perfect to work in GUI environment.
    (ii) Device which can capture real time photos and videos.
    (iii) Device which can convert handwritten text to a digital image.

Answers

For Detailed Solutions
Scan the code

Multiple Choice Questions

1. *(a)*   2. *(b)*   3. *(d)*   4. *(c)*   5. *(a)*   6. *(c)*

CHAPTER 02

Computer Memory

In this Chapter...

- Primary Memory
- Secondary Memory/ Storage Devices
- Basic Units of Measurement
- Parameters of Memory

Computer memory is one of the most important element in a computer system, which is the internal or external storage area and holds the data and instructions during the processing in the form of binary numbers. It also relates to many devices and components that are responsible for storing data and applications on a temporary or a permanent basis.

Computer memory can be classified into two types, which are as follows

Primary Memory

It is also known as **main memory**. It is the internal memory used by computer to hold data, instructions and programs needed at that instant by CPU. It has limited storage capacity, i.e. it requires constant power supply to motion the current information. It is generally made up of semiconductor device.

There are two types of primary memory, which are as follows

1. RAM (Random Access Memory)

RAM is the internal memory that can be accessed (read from as well as written to). This memory is often associated with volatile types of memory.

RAM Chip

It can hold data only on temporary basis because it requires a continuous flow of electrical current. If current is interrupted, data is lost. It is an integrated circuit that enables you to access the stored data in a random order constantly.

The two main forms of RAM are as follows

- **SRAM (Static RAM)** It is a computer memory that requires a constant power flow in order to hold information. It is more expensive which requires more power, therefore it is commonly used in cache and video card memory.

- **DRAM (Dynamic RAM)** It stores information in a cell containing a capacitor and transistor, these cells must be refreshed with electric impulses in few milliseconds. This process allows memory to keep charge which hold the data as long as needed. Also, it is slower than SRAM.

There are some enhanced versions of RAM, which are as follows

- **EDORAM** (Extended Data Output RAM)
- **SDRAM** (Synchronous Dynamic RAM)
- **DDRSDRAM** (Double Data Rate Synchronous Dynamic RAM)

Advantages of RAM

The advantages of RAM are as follows

(i) RAM operation is completely silent, there is no moving part.

(ii) Uses much less power than disk drives.

(iii) Fastest storage medium.

Disadvantages of RAM

The disadvantages of RAM are as follows
  (i) Volatile (temporary) in nature.
  (ii) Limited storage capacity.
  (iii) Much expensive.

2. ROM (Read Only Memory)

In ROM, information once stored remain fixed, i.e. it cannot be changed. So, it can only be read and used. Generally, it contains a set of start-up instructions, i.e. what to do when a computer is turned ON. The contents of ROM remain stored even if power gets turned OFF. This memory is often associated with non-volatile types of memory. It cannot be altered once the chip has been made.

ROM Chip

ROM is further sub-divided into several types, which are as follows

- **PROM (Programmable ROM)** It is a computer memory chip capable of being programmed after it has been created. But, once the PROM has been programmed, the information written is permanent, i.e. it cannot be erased or deleted.
- **EPROM (Erasable Programmable ROM)** It is a computer memory chip on which the written information can be changed by exposing to ultraviolet light. It is just like a small glass circle that exposed the chip that can be reprogrammed.
- **EEPROM (Electrically Erasable Programmable ROM)** It is a PROM that can be erased and reprogrammed using electricity.

Advantages of ROM

The advantages of ROM are as follows
  (i) Non-volatile in nature.
  (ii) Design can be easily changed or modified.
  (iii) Cheaper and more reliable than RAMs.

Disadvantages of ROM

The disadvantages of ROM are as follows
  (i) More power consumption.
  (ii) Data is physically encoded in a circuit, so it can only be programmed during fabrication.
  (iii) It cannot be altered.

Secondary Memory/Storage Devices

It is also known as **Secondary Storage** or **Auxiliary Memory**. It is slower and cheaper form of memory, which is a permanent storage device. CPU does not access the secondary memory directly. The contents in it must be first copied into the RAM to get processed. Secondary memory is non-volatile in nature, i.e. the information does not get erased even when power gets switched OFF and data will not be destructed until and unless, the user erases it.

Devices which are commonly included in the category of secondary memory are shown in following table

Magnetic Disks	Optical Discs	Solid State
Floppy Disk Drive	CD	Pen Drive
Hard Disk Drive	DVD	Memory Stick
Magnetic Tape	Blu-ray Disc	

1. Floppy Disk Drive (FDD)

It is a computer disk drive that enables a user to save data on removable diskettes. This portable storage device is a rewritable media that can be reused number of times. It is made of plastic with magnetic coating on it and round in shape which is covered by square plastic jacket. It is commonly used to move files between different computers. However, this technology is now-a-days become obsolete.

Floppy Disk

Advantages of a Floppy Disk Drive

The advantages of a floppy disk drive are as follows
  (i) Small and light weighted.
  (ii) Inexpensive and reusable.
  (iii) Information is retrieved or accessed only sequentially.

Disadvantages of a Floppy Disk Drive

The disadvantages of a floppy disk drive are as follows
  (i) Can easily to be broken or damaged and not much reliable.
  (ii) Quite slow to access and retrieve data.
  (iii) Easily affected by heat.

2. Hard Disk Drive (HDD)

It is a non-volatile computer storage device containing magnetic disks or platters rotating at high speeds. Non-volatile means data is retained when the computer is turned OFF.

It is a secondary storage device used to store data permanently.

Hard disk drive

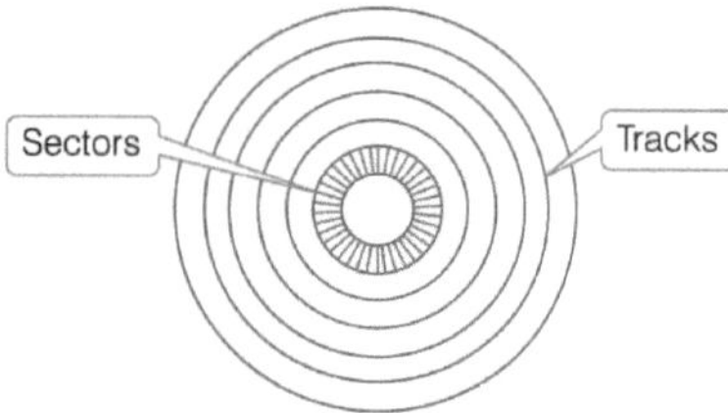

Tracks and sectors

HDD consists of a spindle that holds non-magnetic flat circular disks called **platters**, which hold the recorded data. Each platter requires two read/write heads that is used to write and read the information from a platter. All the read/write heads are attached to a single access **arm**, so that they cannot move independently. The information is recorded in bands, each band of information is called a **track**. Each platter has the same number of tracks and a track location that cuts across all platters is called a **cylinder**. The tracks are divided into pie-shaped sections known as **sectors**.

Advantages of a Hard Disk Drive

The advantages of a hard disk drive are as follows
  (i) Store and retrieve data much faster than a floppy disk.
  (ii) Usually fixed inside the computer, so that do not get lost or damaged easily.
  (iii) Cheap on a cost per megabyte compared to other storage media.

Disadvantages of a Hard Disk Drive

The disadvantages of a hard disk drive are as follows
  (i) Slower than RAM/ROM.
  (ii) Cannot easily be transferred to another computer.

3. Magnetic Tape

It is a storage medium made up of a magnetic material on a large open reel or in a smaller cartridge or cassette (like a musiccassette). It is used for those applications that are based on sequential data processing, i.e. it is a sequential data access medium. Due to this (sequential data access) nature, these tapes are not suitable for data files that need to be revised or updated often. It is generally used to store backup data or that type of data, which is not frequently used or to transfer data from one system to another.

Magnetic tape

Advantages of a Magnetic Tape

The advantages of a magnetic tape are as follows
  (i) Tapes can be erased and reused many times.
  (ii) A large amount of data can be stored in a small storage space.
  (iii) Tape reels and cartridges are compact and light in weight.

Disadvantages of a Magnetic Tape

The disadvantages of a magnetic tape are as follows
  (i) Sequential in nature, not suitable where data is accessed requires a random order.
  (ii) Tape ribbon may get twisted due to wrapping, resulting in loss of stored data.
  (iii) Updating the record is difficult.

4. Compact Disc (CD)

It is an optical media that is used to store digital data. It is relatively cheap storage device. Compact disc is categorised into three main types, which are as follows

- **CD-ROM (CD-Read Only Memory)** Data is recorded permanently on the surface of the optical disc through the use of laser. The recorded content cannot be changed or erased by the users. It is also called **WORM** (Write Once Read Many) disc. It is capable of storing large amount of data upto 1GB, although the most common storage capacity is 700 MB.
- **CD-R (CD-Recordable)** Data can be written on these discs only once. The data once stored in these discs cannot be erased.
- **CD-RW (CD-ReWritable)** It is an erasable disc, which is used to write data multiple times on a disc by the use of format feature.

Advantages of a Compact Disc

The advantages of a compact disc are as follows
  (i) Large storage capacity.
  (ii) Very cheap to produce in large quantities.

Disadvantages of a Compact Disc

The disadvantages of a compact disc are as follows
  (i) Have high access time.
  (ii) It is read only and cannot be updated.

5. Digital Video Disc (DVD)

It is also known as Digital Versatile Disc (DVD) or Super Density Disc (SDD). It is an optical disc storage media manufactured for the first time by Philips, Sony, Toshiba and Panasonic in 1995. It offers high storage capacity than compact disc, while having the same dimensions.

Digital video disc is categorised into three main types, which are as follows

- **DVD-ROM (DVD-Read Only Memory)** A DVD disc used to permanently store data files. These discs are widely used to distribute large software applications that exceed the capacity of a CD-ROM disc.
- **DVD-R (DVD-Recordable)** It is a digital optical disc storage format. It is a DVD that can be written once and read arbitrarily many times and typically has a storage capacity of 4.7 GB.
- **DVD-RW (DVD–ReWritable)** It is a rewritable optical disc with equal storage capacity to a DVD-R, typically 4.7 GB (4,700,000,000 bytes). The smaller Mini DVD-RW holds 1.46 GB with a diameter of 8 cm.

Advantages of a Digital Video Disc

The advantages of a digital video disc are as follows

(i) Superior data storage.
(ii) High density and portability.
(iii) Sound and picture quality are excellent, making them ideal for storing films with video and sound.

Disadvantages of a Digital Video Disc

The disadvantages of a digital video disc are as follows

(i) DVDs do not work in CD drives.
(ii) It can be easily damaged by breaking or scratching.
(iii) It does not fully support HDTV.

6. Blu-ray Disc (BD)

It is an optical disc storage medium designed to recapture data normally in DVD format. It contains 25 GB (23.31 GB) per layer space. The name blu-ray disc refers to the blue laser used to read the disc, which allows information to be stored at a greater density. It can hold almost five times more data than a single layer DVD.

Blu-ray disc is categorised into four main types, which are as follows

- **BD-ROM (BD-Read Only Memory)** It is a high definition optical disc storage format of the blu-ray family that consists of pre-recorded data. It can only read audio and video information.
- **BD-RE (BD–REwritable)** It is a high capacity, high definition optical storage disc format that can withstand multiple erasing and re-recording.
- **BD-R (BD–Recordable)** It is a high capacity optical disc format that can be written only once with audio and video data.

- **BD-RW (BD–ReWritable)** It specifies that PC data on the disc can be re-written many times.

Advantages of a Blu-ray Disc

The advantages of a blu-ray disc are as follows

(i) Large storage capacity.
(ii) Backwards compatibility.
(iii) Mandatory managed copy.

Disadvantages of a Blu-ray Disc

The disadvantages of a blu-ray disc are as follows

(i) Very expensive technology.
(ii) Not widely used by the general public.
(iii) External blu-ray drives are expensive and unwieldy.

7. Pen/Flash/Thumb Drive

It is a data storage device that consists of flash memory (USB memory/key memory) with an integrated, Universal Serial Bus (USB) interface. USB flash drives are typically removable, rewritable and physically much smaller than a floppy disk.

A USB flash drive or data stick is a portable drive that is same as the size of your thumb that connects to the computer USB port. Today, flash drives are available in various storage capacities as 256 MB, 512 MB, 1 GB, 2 GB, 4 GB, 16 GB, 64 GB etc. It is widely used as an easy and small medium to transfer and store the information from the computers.

Pen drives

Advantages of Pen/Flash/Thumb Drive

The advantages of pen drive are as follows

(i) Data read/write is faster as compared to traditional hard disk drives.
(ii) It uses little power and have no fragile moving parts.
(iii) It also stores data densely compared to many removable media.
(iv) It is smaller in size.

Disadvantages of Pen/Flash/Thumb Drive

The disadvantages of pen drive are as follows

(i) Limited number of write and erase cycles before failing.
(ii) Easy to mislay because of its smaller size.
(iii) Most flash drives do not have a write protection mechanism.

8. Memory Stick

It is a physically different form of memory card from SD. It is an USB based flash memory drive. A family of flash memory cards from Sony designed for digital storage in camera, camcorders and other handheld devices. Capacity of memory stick varies from 4 MB to 256 MB. Its average transfer rate is 2.45 MB/s, write rate is 1.5 MB/s, average power consumption is 45 mA and in standby mode is 130 μA. Memory stick comes in various varieties, which are as follows

- **PRO** The Memory Stick PRO, introduced in 2003 as a joint effort between Sony and ScanDisk. It has high transfer speed and a maximum storage capacity of 32 GB. All Memory Stick PROs larger than 1 GB support high speed mode.
- **DuO** It is a small flash memory card developed for digital camera, cell phones etc. It is a smaller version of memory stick.
- **MagicGate** It was introduced by Sony in 1994, as a copy–protection technology. It encrypts the data on the device and using MagicGate chips, reader controls over how the files are copied on the device.

Advantages of a Memory Stick

The advantages of a memory stick are as follows

- (i) It allows more immediate access.
- (ii) It has relatively large storage space compared to old backup devices.
- (iii) It is a USB drive, thus it can be used on any computer system.

Disadvantages of a Memory Stick

The disadvantages of a memory stick are as follows

- (i) It can be break and lost easily.
- (ii) These cards may get affected by electronic corruption.
- (iii) Cannot be attached or read on the computer without proper hardware unlike pen drive.

Primary versus Secondary Memory

Volatile Primary memory is both volatile and non-volatile in nature whereas secondary memory is non-volatile in nature.

Accessible Primary memory is directly accessible by the CPU whereas secondary memory is not.

Position Primary memory is situated inside the CPU but secondary memory may be attached externally or internally.

Storage Space Primary memory has a limited storage space, whereas secondary memory has virtually infinite space to run and stores bulk of data.

Basic Units of Measurement

When user uses a RAM, ROM, Floppy disk, Hard disk etc., the data is measured using some units. In computer terminology, they are called Nibble, Bit, Byte, Kilobyte, Gigabyte etc.

Units of computer memory measurement are as follows

- **Bit** (Binary digit) The smallest unit of data. It is either 0 or 1.
- **Nibble** A group of 4 bits or half a byte.
- **Byte** A group of 8 bits. A byte can represent 256 (2^8) distinct values, such as the integers from 0 to 255. Each keyboard character is represented through atleast 1 byte.
- **Kilobyte** (KB) It is actually 2^{10} bytes or 1 KB = 1024 bytes.
- **Megabyte** (MB) It is actually 2^{20} bytes or 1 MB = 1024 KB.
- **Gigabyte** (GB) It is actually 2^{30} bytes or 1 GB = 1024 MB.
- **Terabyte** (TB) It is actually 2^{40} bytes or 1 TB = 1024 GB.
- **Petabyte** (PB) It is actually 2^{50} bytes or 1 PB = 1024 TB.
- **Exabyte** (EB) It is actually 2^{60} bytes or 1 EB = 1024 PB.
- **Zettabyte** (ZB) It is actually 2^{70} bytes or 1 ZB = 1024 EB.
- **Yottabyte** (YB) It is actually 2^{80} bytes or 1 YB = 1024 ZB.
- **Brontobyte** It is actually 2^{90} bytes or 1 Brontobyte = 1024 YB.
- **Geopbyte** It is actually 2^{100} bytes or 1 Geopbyte = 1024 Brontobyte.

Parameters of Memory

The following terms are most commonly used for identifying comparative behaviour of various memory devices and technologies

- **Storage Capacity** It represents the size of the memory. The capacity of internal memory and main memory can be expressed in terms of numbers of words or bytes.
- **Access Modes** A memory is comprised of various memory locations. The information from these memory locations can be accessed randomly, sequentially and directly.
- **Access Time** It is the time required between the desired modes for a read or write operation till the data is made available or written at the desired location.
- **Physical Characteristics** In this respect, the devices can be categorised into four main categories, i.e. electronic, magnetic mechanical and optical.
- **Permanence of Storage** Its permanency is high for future in magnetic or optical materials.
- **Throughput** It defines the amount of information exchanged per unit of time, expressed in bits per second.
- **Cycle Time** It represents the minimal time interval between two successive accesses.

Chapter Practice

Objective Questions

• Multiple Choice Questions

1. Out of these, which one is a volatile memory?
(a) ROM   (b) RAM
(c) Floppy   (d) DVD

Ans. (*b*) RAM is called as temporary or volatile memory because it can store data or information only till the power is ON.

2. Which of the following is an example of non-volatile memory?
(a) ROM   (b) RAM   (c) LSI   (d) VLSI

Ans. (*a*) ROM is a non-volatile memory because the instructions stores inside ROM are stored permanently and used at the time of booting process.

3. .... memory is used to store large amount of information permanently.
(a) RAM   (b) ROM
(c) Secondary   (d) Primary

Ans. (*c*) There are two types of memories in computer-primary and secondary. The primary memory stores limited data and only temporarily while secondary memory can be larger as possible and stores data permanently.

4. Which is not a type of ROM?
(a) PROM   (b) EPROM
(c) DROM   (d) EEPROM

Ans. (*c*) The ROM is of three types only – PROM, EPROM and EEPROM.

5. Size of the memory is also referred as .... capacity.
(a) stack   (b) storage
(c) buffer   (d) All of these

Ans. (*b*) Every type of memory in computer is called as storage and have a predefined capacity. Therefore, the capacity of memory is called as storage capacity.

6. .... memory does not deal directly with the CPU.
(a) RAM   (b) ROM
(c) Keyboard   (d) Secondary

Ans. (*d*) Secondary memory does not deal directly with the CPU. The contents in it must be first coped into the RAM to get processed.

7. There are two types of computer memory .... and ....·
(a) hard disk, primary
(b) printer, ROM
(c) RAM, ROM
(d) primary, secondary

Ans. (*d*) Computer has two types of memory internal and external. Internal memory is called as primary memory also called as memory unit and external memory is called as secondary memory.

8. EPROM is called as
(a) Erase Program ROM
(b) Eatable Programmable ROM
(c) Erasable Programmable ROM
(d) Easy Programmable ROM

Ans. (*c*) EPROM is called as Erasable Programmable ROM.

9. The data can be .... accessed from RAM.
(a) serial   (b) randomly
(c) sequential   (d) block

Ans. (*b*) The RAM is called a Random Access Memory, means the data can be randomly accessed from RAM.

10. The .... offers more than five times the storage capacity of traditional DVDs.
(a) compact disc   (b) pen drive
(c) blu-ray disc   (d) ext-DVD

Ans. (*c*) Blu-ray disc is an optical disc storage medium designed to recapture data normally in DVD format. It contains 25 GB (23.31 GB) per layer space. The name blu-ray disc refers to the blue laser used to read the disc, which allows information to be stored at a greater density. It can hold almost five times more data than a single layer DVD.

11. Pen drive is also known as
    (a) USB flash drive   (b) data stick
    (c) thumb drive   (d) All of these

Ans. (a) It is a data storage device that consists of flash memory (USB memory/key memory) with an integrated Universal Serial Bus (USB) interface. USB flash drives are typically removable, rewritable and physically much smaller than a floppy disk.

12. The largest unit of memory is
    (a) Terabyte (b) Petabyte   (b) Exabyte   (d) Geopbyte

Ans. (d) Geopbyte is the highest memory measurement unit. It is equal to 1024 Brontobyte (nearly 2^{100} bytes).

13. Which of the following statement is false?
    (a) Secondary storage is faster.
    (b) Primary storage is both volatile and non-volatile in nature.
    (c) When the computer is turned OFF, data and instructions stored in RAM are erased.
    (d) None of the above

Ans. (a) There are two types of memory in computers. Primary and secondary. Primary memory is a part of CPU, therefore faster than secondary memory. Secondary memory is attached externally.

14. Which of the following storage device can be used for storing large backup data?
    (a) Floppy disk   (b) Hard disk
    (c) Magnetic tape   (d) None of these

Ans. (c) It is a storage medium made up of a magnetic material on a large open reel or in a smaller cartridge or cassette (like a music cassette). The main advantage of this device is it can store large amount of data in small space.

• Case Based MCQs

Direction *Read the case and answer the following questions.*

15. Drishti, Mohan, Ram, Niti and Harish are Class 9th students and friends. Drishti purchased a new laptop. All friends are exploring her laptop and wants to do the next assignments in her laptop only. They are checking specification of the laptop written on the laptop box. It says it has 1TB hard disk, 4 GB RAM, 2 GHZ processor, keyboard and a screen. Some specification of ROM is also given. Niti is looking for video card and she finds that laptop has no separate RAM for video card. All friends are having various questions in their mind.

    (i) The laptop has three type of memory. Which type of memory can be used for storing data permanently?
        (a) RAM   (b) ROM
        (c) Secondary memory   (d) Primary memory

    (ii) Mohan and Ram are confused with ROM and secondary memory. Ram is asking to Mohan, when ROM can save data permanently, then why do I need to have hard disk? Choose appropriate reason Mohan has specified.
        (a) Data on ROM can be written with some specific techniques only.
        (b) ROM has a limited size.
        (c) ROM data cannot be copied and accessed by users normally.
        (d) All of the above

    (iii) Drishti is asking to teacher "mam I need to purchase a RAM for my video card in computer. Can you suggest me which RAM I should purchase"?
        (a) SRAM   (b) DRAM   (c) SDRAM (d) Any one

    (iv) Harish is confused about the specification 4GB RAM.
        (a) It defines the size of RAM in Gega Bytes.
        (b) It defines speed of RAM.
        (c) It defines the amount of time consumed to access data from RAM.
        (d) All of the above

    (v) Niti asked a question from Drishti, what is the full form of TB?
        (a) Teen Byte   (b) Tera Byte
        (c) Tetra Byte   (d) Tara Byte

Ans. (i) (c) Hard disk can be used to store data permanently. As this is a type of secondary memory.

    (ii) (d) In ROM, information is stored once, and remain fixed which cannot be changed. But in hard disk we can store information and changed it wherever required.

    (iii) (a) SRAM (Static RAM) is a computer memory that requires a constant power flow in order to hold information. It is more expensive which requires more power, therefore it is commonly used in cache and video card memory.

    (iv) (a) GB is used a unit to specify size of the memory. Therefore, 4GB is a storage capacity, i.e. size or RAM.

    (v) (b) The TB is a unit to measure the capacity of a memory. It is called as Tera Byte and 1 TB.

16. Secondary storage is an external memory attached in computer. It is also called as **Auxiliary Memory**. The working speed of secondary memory is slower than other primary memory. Also, it is a cheaper form of memory, which is also called as permanent storage device. CPU does not access the secondary memory directly. The contents of secondary memory required to be first copied into the RAM for processing. Secondary memory is non-volatile in nature, i.e. the information does not get erased even when power gets switched OFF and data will not be lost until and unless, the user deletes it. Some popularly used secondary storage devices are – Hard disk, Pen drive and Memory stick.

Hard disk is a type of random access digital data storage device, which is used for storing and retrieving digital information using rotating disks called as platters, coated with magnetic material. All programs of a computer are installed in hard disk within a particular drive.

Pen drive is also called as flash drive. It is a data storage device that consists of flash memory (USB memory/key memory) with an integrated Universal Serial Bus (USB) interface. It is widely used as an easy and small medium to transfer and store the information from the computers.

Memory stick is basically used in digital cameras to store data of a digital camera.

(i) In comparison to primary memory, secondary memory is .... to computer.
  (a) internal   (b) external
  (c) attached with monitor   (d) attached with CPU

(ii) Now-a-days most commonly used external memories are Hard disk, Memory stick and ....
  (a) Floppy disk   (b) Magnetic tape
  (c) Pen drive   (d) CD-ROM

(iii) In hard disk, the information can be store or access using rotating disk called as
  (a) magnet   (b) platter
  (c) shaft   (d) rod

(iv) Whenever user wish to install any program then installed program can be stored only in
  (a) RAM   (b) ROM
  (c) hard disk   (d) pen drive

(v) Flash memory is also called as
  (a) Memory stick   (b) Hard disk
  (c) Floppy   (d) Pen drive

Ans. (i) (*b*) Secondary storage is an external memory attached in computer. It is also called as **Auxiliary Memory**.

(ii) (*c*) Some popularly used secondary storage devices are – Hard disk, Memory stick and Pen drive.

(iii) (*b*) Hard disk is a random access digital data storage device, which is used for storing and retrieving digital information using rotating disks (platters) coated with magnetic material.

(iv) (*c*) All programs of a computer are installed in hard disk within a particular drive.

(v) (*d*) Flash drive is also called as pen dreive. It is a data storage device that consists of flash memory (USB memory/key memory) with an integrated Universal Serial Bus (USB) interface.

PART 2
Subjective Questions

• Short Answer Type Questions

1. Differentiate between SRAM and DRAM.

Ans. Differences between SRAM and DRAM are as follows

SRAM	DRAM
It is called as Static RAM.	It is called as Dynamic RAM.
Data is stored in transistors and requires a constant power flow.	Capacitors that store data in DRAM gradually discharge energy, no energy means the data has been lost.
Faster than DRAM.	Slower than SRAM.

2. What are the advantages of RAM?

Ans. The advantages of RAM are as follows

(i) RAM operation is completely silent, there is no moving part.

(ii) Uses much less power than disk drives.

(iii) Fastest storage medium.

3. What are the types of ROM?

Ans. ROM is called as Read Only Memory. There are three main types of the ROM, which are as follows

(i) **PROM (Programmable ROM)** It is a type of ROM which can be programmed after it has been created. But, once it is programmed, the information written on it becomes permanent, means cannot be deleted or updated further.

(ii) **EPROM (Erasable Programmable ROM)** It is a type of ROM on which the written information can be changed or updated by exposing the ultraviolet light on it. It is just like a small glass circle that exposed the chip that can be reprogrammed.

(iii) **EEPROM (Electrically Erasable Programmable ROM)** It is a PROM that can be erased and reprogrammed using electricity.

4. Differentiate between RAM and ROM.

Ans. Differences between RAM and ROM are as follows

RAM	ROM
RAM is a volatile memory, which could store the data as long as the power is supplied.	ROM is a non-volatile memory, which could retain the data even when power is turned OFF.
Used to store the data that has to be currently processed by CPU temporarily.	It stores the instructions required during booting of the computer.

5. The computer memory relates to many devices and components.

(i) What do you mean by memory?

(ii) How many types of memory the computer has?

Ans. (i) Computer memory enables a person to retain the information that is stored on the computer.

(ii) Computer has basically two types of memory as follows

Internal memory Main memory units (RAM and ROM) and cache memory.

External memory Secondary memory.

6. Name the storage device whose contents have to be erased completely every time when a user wants to change or add some data.

Ans. **CD-RW** (Compact Disc-Rewritable) is a storage device whose contents have to be completely erased every time when a user wants to change or add some data. A CD-RW can be written multiple number of times. The data burned on a CD-RW cannot be changed, but it can be erased.

7. Sonam is a computer engineer in ABC Company. She has one newly appointed assistant. Sonam is giving training to the assistant and explains the structure of the hard disk. She says that, hard disk is a non-volatile which can be used as random access digital data storage device. It can be used as input device as well as output device. When we are required to read some data it behaves as an input device. The data that we read from it, transfers to RAM a volatile memory and then process by CPU. When we store something on disk, it behaves as output device. Further, she explains that the hard disk works with a device called as Hard Disk Drive (HDD). The HDD consists of a spindle that holds non-magnetic flat circular disks called platters. Each platter requires two read/write heads that is used to write and read the information from a platter.

(i) How the hard disk can be considered as input as well as output device both?

(ii) What is platter in hard disk drive?

Ans. (i) When we are required to read some data it behaves as an input device. The data that we read from it, transfers to RAM a volatile memory and then process by CPU. When we store something on disk it behaves as output device.

(ii) The HDD consists of a spindle that holds non-magnetic flat circular disks called platters. Each platter requires two read/write heads that is used to write and read the information from a platter.

• Long Answer Type Questions

8. The ABC Company has opened his office in Delhi. The main work of ABC Company is to develop software as per the requirement of a customer. Before COVID-19 pandemic all employees use to come office and use to work from office only using Desktop computers allocated in company. But during COVID-19 the office got closed and all employees asked to work from home and required to complete all assignments. Soha is a front desk employee of a company and has no computer in her home. Now, she wants to buy a new computer. She wants to use this system in her home as well as in office too. She visited some websites to purchase computer online. But she is not able to understand the terminology used in the specifications, such as 2GB RAM, 500GB Hard disk, 1.8 GHZ processor, etc. Also, she is confused what kind of benefit she will get in future after spending so much money to purchase computer.

(i) Which type of computer Soha should purchase? What kind of memory device she should purchase to carry her work from one place to another?

(ii) Explain the meaning of specification given on the website –2GB RAM, 500GB Hard disk, 1.8 GHZ processor.

Ans. (i) She should purchase one pen drive, so that she can store her files of work and carry from one place to another.

(ii) The smallest unit to measure the storage capacity of a memory is bit. Following is a table of storage unit and conversion

Unit (Symbol)	Value (SI)
Kilobyte (KB)	10^3
Megabyte (MB)	10^6
Gigabyte (GB)	10^9
Terabyte (TB)	10^{12}
Petabyte (PB)	10^{15}
Exabyte (EB)	10^{18}
Zettabyte (ZB)	10^{21}
Yottabyte (YB)	10^{24}

2GB RAM means primary memory capacity is 2 Gigabytes.

500 GB Hard disk means the secondary or permanent memory given in laptop is 500 Gigabytes

1.8 GHZ processor The speed of CPU is measured in MHZ. GHZ is the bigger unit than that (1 GHZ= 1000 MHZ).

9. Explain all the parameters used for computer memory.

Ans. **Parameters of Memory** The following terms are most commonly used for identifying comparative behaviour of various memory devices and technologies

(i) **Storage Capacity** It represents the size of the memory. The capacity of internal memory and main memory can be expressed in terms of numbers of words or bytes.

(ii) **Access Modes** A memory is comprised of various memory locations. The information from these memory locations can be accessed randomly, sequentially and directly.

(iii) **Access Time** It is the time required between the desired modes for a read or write operation till the data is made available or written at the desired location.

(iv) **Physical Characteristics** In this respect, the devices can be categorised into four main categories, i.e. electronic, magnetic, mechanical and optical.

(v) **Permanence of Storage** Its permanency is high for future in magnetic or optical materials.

(vi) **Throughput** It defines the amount of information exchanged per unit of time, expressed in bits per second.

(vii) **Cycle Time** It represents the minimal time interval between two successive accesses.

10. Explain hard disk drive as secondary storage device. Also, explain its advantages and disadvantages.

Ans. Hard disk is a non-volatile, random access digital data storage device which is used for storing and retrieving digital information. It uses multiple rotating disks called as platters. These platters are coated with magnetic material. All programs of a computer are installed in hard disk within a particular drive. HDD consists of a spindle that holds non-magnetic flat circular disks called platters. The platters hold the recorded data. Each platter requires two read/write heads on both side. These heads area used to write and read the information from a platter. All the read/write heads are attached to a single access arm, so that they cannot move independently. The information is recorded in bands. These band area called as tracks. Each platter has the same number of tracks and a track location that cuts across all platters is called a cylinder. The tracks are divided into pie-shaped sections known as sectors.

The advantages of a hard disk drive are as follows

(i) Store and retrieve data much faster than a floppy disk.

(ii) Usually fixed inside the computer so do not get lost or damaged easily.

(iii) Cheap on a cost per megabyte compared to other storage media.

The disadvantages of a hard disk drive are as follows

(i) Slower than RAM/ROM.

(ii) Cannot easily be transferred to another computer.

Chapter Test

Multiple Choice Questions

1. In which type of memory, once the program or data is written, it cannnot be changed?
(a) Programmable ROM
(b) Eatable Programmable ROM
(c) Erasable Programmable ROM
(d) Easy Programmable ROM

2. The .... is a storage device which offers more than five times storage capacity in comparison to traditional DVDs.
(a) compact disc
(b) pen drive
(c) blu-ray disc
(d) ext-DVD

3. Mohan is a computer operator. He wants to save his data permanently in such as way so that no one can easily modifies it. Suggest, which device he can use it?
(a) Hard disk
(b) Floppy
(c) CD-ROM
(d) Pen drive

4. The floppy disk is made up of .... material.
(a) magnetic
(b) plastic
(c) tin
(d) iron

5. The capacity of 5.25 inch floppy is .... KB.
(a) 5000
(b) 120
(c) 525
(d) 1200

6. Which type of memory is primarily used by computer for booting of the system?
(a) Primary memory
(b) Secondary memory
(c) Both (a) and (b)
(d) None of these

Short Answer Type Questions

7. Explain the use of RAM in computers.

8. What is the main purpose of ROM?

9. What is the difference between primary memory and secondary memory?

10. What are the advantages of ROM ?

11. Write the difference between hard disk and pen drive.

Long Answer Type Questions

12. Explain the purpose of following I/O or storage devices – Webcam, Memory stick and Magnetic Tape.

13. Describe the use of memory stick.

Answers

Multiple Choice Questions

1. (a)　　*2. (c)*　　*3. (c)*　　*4. (b)*　　*5. (d)*　　*6. (a)*

For Detailed Solutions
Scan the code

CHAPTER 03

Computer Software

In this Chapter...

- Classification of Software
- System Software
- Application Software
- Mobile Applications

Software is a set of computer programs, procedures and associated documentation concerned with the operation of a data processing system. Software commonly known as programs, consists of all required instructions that tell the hardware how to perform a task. It is not only basic requirement of a computer system but, it makes a computer more powerful and useful.

Classification of Software

Software can be broadly classified into two major categories, which are as follows

1. System software   2. Application software

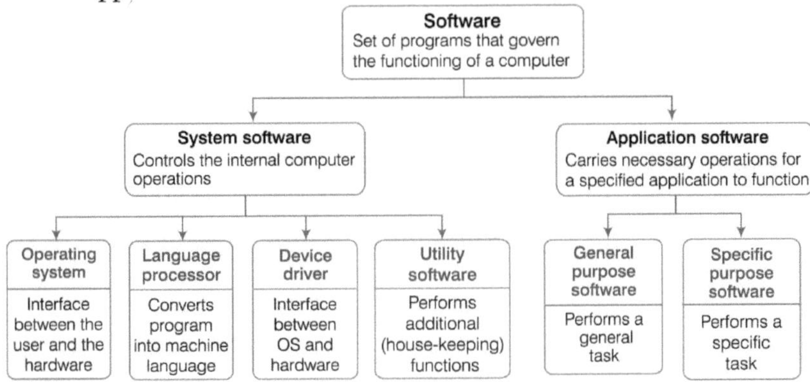

Classification of software

1. System Software

All those programs which are used by a computer system either for its activation or internal resource management are called system software. *For example*, software that would transfer the data/instructions from input devices to computer's memory will be a system software. It refers to the programs that control internal computer operations and makes best use of the hardware devices.

System software can be classified into various categories, which are as follows

(i) Operating System (OS)

It is a program that acts as an interface between the user and the hardware (i.e. for all computer resources). An operating system is an important component of a computer system, which controls and co-ordinates all other components of it. It activates all devices that make them ready for work. It also performs all internal management functions and ensures systematic functioning of a computer system. The computer's OS is a well-known example of system software.

The operating system performs the following functions

- It recognises input from keyboard and sends output to the display screen.
- It makes sure that the programs running simultaneously do not interfere with each other.
- It is also responsible for security, ensuring that unauthorised users cannot access the system. e.g. MS-DOS, Windows 95, Windows XP, Windows Vista, etc.

Also, as per the user interface operating system can be classified into two categories : Character User Interface (CUI) and Graphical User Interface (GUI). In CUI, OS requires the users to interact with OS by typing each and every command, while GUI based OS provides the command in the form of icons and menus. e.g. DOS is CUI and Windows is GUI OS.

(ii) Device Driver

The software which is written with the objective of making a device functional, when the device is connected to the computer system is called device driver or simply driver. A device driver is a system software that acts as an interface between the device and the user or an operating system.

All computer accessories like : printer, scanner, web camera etc., have their own driver software. This software helps an operating system and other application software to communicate with a particular device for optimal use. Devices from different manufacturers work in different ways. *For example*, Without drivers, the computer could not send and receive data correctly to/from hardware devices, such as a printer. Printers from different companies need different drivers to do work.

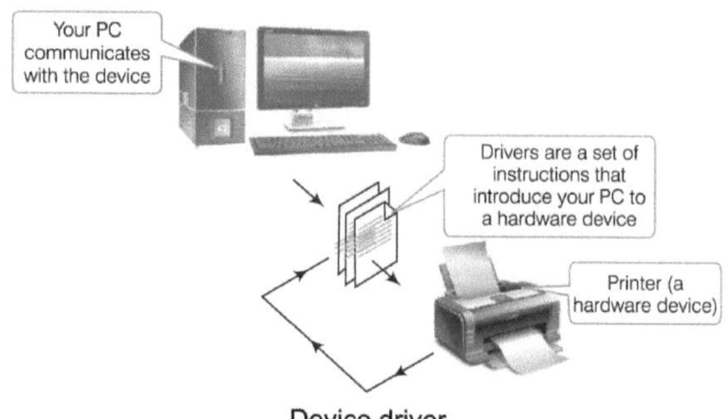

Device driver

When user buys a new hardware, the manufacturer of the hardware provides an installation disk along with it. The user simply needs to load that disk into the computer. After this process, that particular device can be used. Apart from this, drivers can also be downloaded from Internet. But these days, some new operating system like : Windows Vista, Windows 7, etc., are already pre-equipped with many device drivers. So, a user simply needs to plug the device in computer and it works perfectly as its driver is already installed in computer. But, it is possible for some commonly used devices only.

(iii) Language Processors

Language processor are system software which are used for the language translation. We know that, computer understand only machine language (0 and 1), but the user gives the instructions in either high level language or low level language which means the computer cannot understand the instructions directly given by the user. The programs which are written by user in high level language such as : C, C++, Java or Python are called as source code. The source code cannot be executed directly by the computer. Therefore, it is required to be converted in machine language to execute it. To do so, computer needs language translators called as language processors.

Every type of language has its own translator but we can classified them in three categories, which are as follows

- **Compiler** It converts high level language program into machine language, which can be understood by the processor. For each high level language, the machine requires a separate compiler. Languages in which compiler used are C, C++, Java, etc.

Source code ⟶ Compiler ⟶ Object code
(High level language) (Machine language)

- **Interpreter** The language processor that converts each statement of the source program into machine code and executes it immediately before the conversion of the next statement.

Languages in which interpreter used are Python, Ruby, etc.

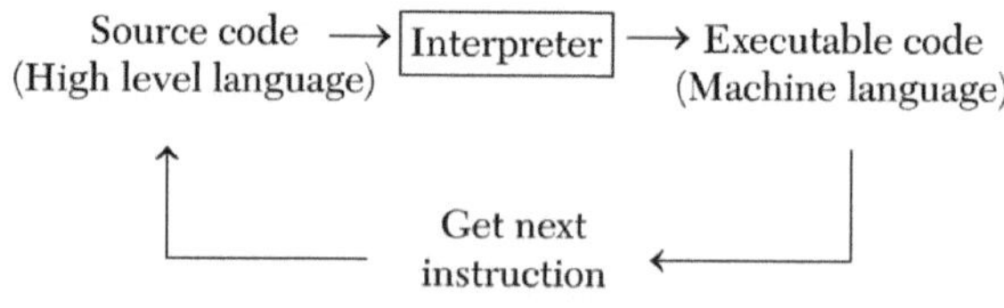

Source code ⟶ Interpreter ⟶ Executable code
(High level language) (Machine language)

Get next instruction

- **Assembler** It is a language processor which is used to translate the program written in low level language also called as an assembly language. It works in similar way as compiler.

Source code ⟶ Assembler ⟶ Object code
(Assembly language) (Machine language)

(iv) Utility Software

Utility software are specially designed system software to help users in tuning of computer hardware and software. Utilities programs assist a computer by performing housekeeping functions like disc/folder/file management such as creating, moving, renaming and deleting files. Utility backup software helps is taking backups of the secondary storage time-to-time.

System utility mainly consists of the following functions

- **Disk Compression** It increases the amount of information that can be stored on a hard disk by compressing all information stored on it.
  For example, DiskDoubler, SuperStor Pro, DoubleDisk Gold , etc.

- **Disk Fragmenter** It detects computer files whose contents are broken across several locations on the hard disk and moves the fragments to one location to increase efficiency.
  It can be used to rearrange files and unused space on your hard disk.
  For example, MyDefrag, Diskeeper, Defraggler, etc.

- **Backup Utilities** It can make a copy of all information stored on a disk and restore either the entire disk or selected files.

- **Disk Cleaners** It is used to find files that have not been used for a long time. This utility also serves to increase the speed of a slow computer.
  For example, Bleach Bit cleaner, etc.

- **Anti-virus** It is the utility which is used to scan computer for viruses and prevent the computer system and files from being corrupt.
  For example, Kaspersky, AVG, McAfee, Avira, etc.

- **Text Editor** It is a program that facilitates the creation and correction of text. A text editor supports special commands for text editing, i.e. you can write, delete, find and replace words, lines, paragraphs, etc.
  For example, MS-Word, WordPad, Notepad, etc., in which Notepad is the most popular text editor.

2. Application Software

It is a computer software designed to help the user to perform single or multiple tasks. It acts as a set of instructions, which direct the hardwares to perform specific functions. *For example,* accounting software, office suites, graphics software, media players, etc.

Application softwares are categorised into two main parts as follows

(i) General Purpose Application Software

It is a software, which is used for any general function. It allows people to do simple computer tasks. General purpose software is sometimes referred to as GPS.

Some common general purpose application software are as follows

- **Word Processing Software** It is a software program capable of creating, storing and printing documents. Unlike the standard typewriter, users are using such word processors which have the ability to create a document that make changes anywhere in the document. This document can also be saved for modification, later on or to be opened on any other computer using the same word processor with the help frequently used programs on a computer system.
  For example, MS-Word, WordPerfect, AppleWorks, OpenOffice.org Writer etc.

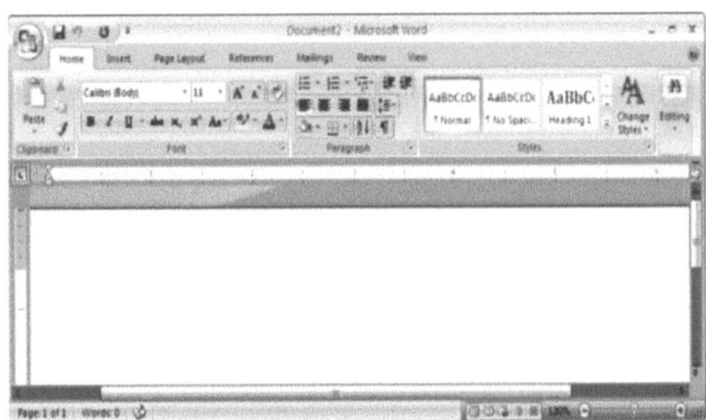

MS-Word window

- **Presentation Software** It is the practice of showing and explaining the contents of a topic to an audience or learner visually. People in a variety of settings and situations, use presentation software to make their presentations more interesting and professional.
  For example, marketing managers use presentation graphics to present new marketing strategies to their superiors.

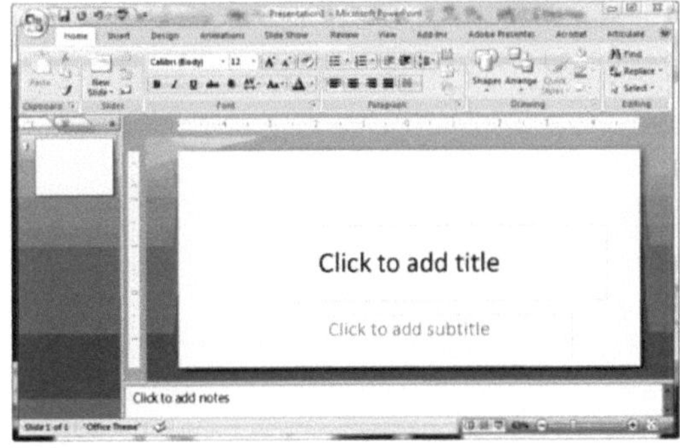

MS-Power-Point window

- **Electronic Spreadsheets** Spreadsheet applications (sometimes referred to simply as spreadsheets) are the computer programs that accept data in a tabular form and allow a user to create and manipulate spreadsheets electronically. In a spreadsheet application, each value exists in a cell. User can define what type of data is in each cell and how the different cells depend on one another. A cell is a box in which you can enter a single piece of data. The relationships between cells are called **formulas** and the names of the cells are called **labels**.

For example, MS-Excel, Quattro Pro, Lotus 1-2-3, OpenOffice.org Calc etc.

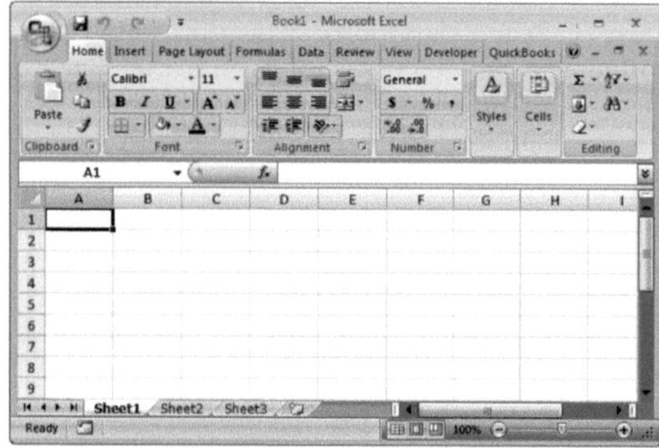

MS-Excel window

- **Database Management System (DBMS)** It refers to the software that is responsible for storing, maintaining and utilising a database. It enables a user to define, create and maintain the database and provides controlled access on it. A database is a collection of integrated data stored together to serve multiple applications.

  For example, MS-Access, Corel Paradox, Lotus Approach, MySQL, OpenOffice.org Base etc.

  Database Management System (DBMS) provides several additional features, which are as follows
  - Removes data redundancy
  - Elimination of data inconsistency
  - Data integration
  - Data sharing
  - Data security

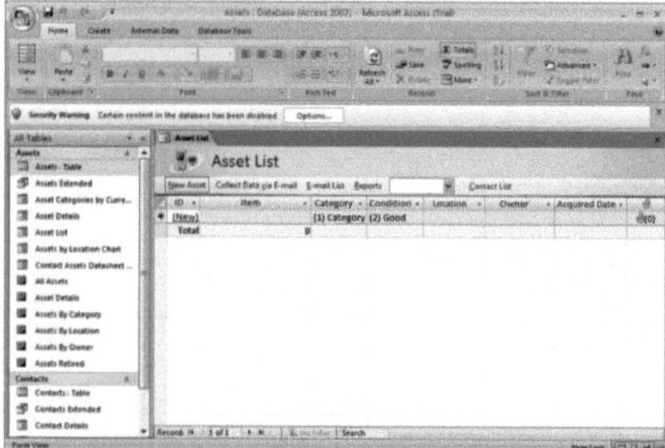

MS-Access window

- **Desktop Publishing (DTP) Software** It is a tool for graphic designers and non-designers to create visual communications for professional. A complete DTP software involves the combination of type setting (choosing fonts and the text layout), graphic design, page layout (how it fits on the page) and print the document.

DTP softwares are used for book publishing, creating leaflets, posters, business cards etc.

e.g. QuarkXPress, Adobe PageMaker, 3B2, CorelDRAW, Corel Ventura, Illustrator etc.

- **Graphics Software (Image Editing)** It is an application program or collection of programs that enables a person to manipulate visual images on a computer system. In other words, these softwares are used to manipulate images that can be used at home, schools or a business.

  Most graphics softwares have the ability to import and export one or more graphic file formats. Typical graphics software enables data to be plotted as line chart, bar chart and pie chart.

  e.g. Adobe Photoshop, piZap, Microsoft Publisher, Picasa etc.

- **Multimedia Software** Multimedia includes a combination of text, audio, images, animations, videos or interactivity content forms.

  In simple words, this software allows user to use a mixture of sound, pictures, films and writing is known as multimedia software. The term is used in contrast to media which uses only elementary computer display such as text only or traditional forms of printed or hand produced material.

  e.g. Flash, Xilisoft Video Converter, VLC Media Player, Nimbuzz etc.

- **Browser** A browser (or web browser) is an application software that is used to retrieve, present and traverse the information resources on the WWW (World Wide Web). The information resource is identified by a Uniform Resource Identifier (URI) and may be a web page, image, video or other piece of content.

  e.g. Lynx, Google Chrome, Mozilla Firefox, Microsoft Internet Explorer, Opera etc.

(ii) Specific Purpose Application Software

It is a type of software, created to execute one specific task. These softwares are called specific purpose application softwares because they target or address a very narrow solution to a problem. It may also be created in house and tailored to the specific needs of a user. The type of software developed to meet particular user specified requirements also falls into this category.

Some of the specific purpose application softwares are as follows

- **Inventory Management System and Purchasing System** It is an attempt to balance inventory needs and requirement to minimise total cost, resulting from obtaining and holding an inventory. Inventory is a list of goods and materials available in a stock. Inventory management system is generally used in departmental stores or in an organisation to keep the records of the stock of all the physical resources. Modern inventory management systems must have the ability to track sales and available inventory, communicate with suppliers in real-time, receive and incorporate other data, such as seasonal demand.

For example, Fishbowl, AdvancePro, etc.

- **Payroll Management System** It is used by all modern organisations to encompass every employee of the organisation, who receives regular wages or other compensation. All different payment methods are calculated by the payroll software and the appropriate pay checks are issued. This software can also be used for printing or E-mailing the salary slip of employees. *For example,* Namely, UltiPro, etc.

- **Hotel Management System** It refers to the management techniques used in the hotel sector. It includes hotel administration, accounts, billing marketing, housekeeping, front office or front desk.

  For example, Hotelogix PMS, DJUBO, True Hotel Management, Aatithya HMS etc.

- **Reservation System or Central Reservation System (CRS)** It is a computerised system used to store and retrieve information and conduct transactions related to air travel, hotels, car rental or other activities. Reservation system is an application software which is commonly seen at railway reservation offices, this software helps the concerned department to automatically check the availability of the seats or berths of any train and on any particular date with an incomparable speed. Today, number of websites like : www.yatra.com, www.makemytrip.com provide online booking for tourists.

- **Accounting Software** This system records and processes accounting transactions within functional modules such as accounts payable, accounts receivable, payroll and trial balance. It works as an accounting information system. e.g. Tally. ERP 9, HDPOS, MARG, ProfitBooks etc. There are several types of accounting software as follows
  - Accounts payable software
  - Bank reconciliation software
  - Budget management software

- **HR Management System** It refers to the systems and processes at the intersection between Human Resource Management (HRM) and Information Technology (IT). The function of HR department is generally administrative and common in all organisations.

- **Attendance System** It is an application software designed to track and optimise the presence of a person/student in an organisation/school. Now-a-days, attendance system can be integrated with customer's existing time/ attendance recording devices like Biometrics/Access cards. Attendance management can be done in two ways as follows

  - Biometric integration
  - Manual attendance integration

  e.g. eTimeTrackLite, Pyramid PTR 4000 etc.

- **Billing System** It refers to the software that is used to perform the billing process. It handles the tracking of labelled products and services delivered to a customer or set of customers.

e.g. Billing Manager, BillingTracker, kBilling etc.

Mobile Applications

Mobile applications (also known as mobile apps) are software programs developed for mobile devices such as smartphones and tablets. They turn mobile devices into miniature powerhouses of function and fun. Some devices come preloaded with some mobile app courtesy of their manufacturers or the mobile service providers with which they are associated (*For example,* Verizon, AT&T, T-Mobile etc.), but many more apps are available through device specific app stores.

Mobile apps are move away from the integrated software systems generally found on PCs. Instead, each app provides limited and isolated functionality such as game, calculator or mobile web browsing. The simplest mobile take PC-based applications and port them to a mobile device. As mobile apps become more robust, this technique is somewhat lacking.

Mobile App Functions

The purpose of these apps to fulfil the various type of requirements from utility, productivity and navigation to entertainment, sports, fitness, etc. Social media is one of the most popular fields of mobile app development and adoption.

In fact, Facebook and Whatsapp are the most widely used app across all platforms. Many online entities have both mobile websites and mobile apps. In general, the difference lies in purpose: An app is usually smaller in scope than a mobile website, offers more interactivity.

Types of Mobile Apps

There are six main types of mobile apps, which are as follows

(i) **Lifestyle Mobile Apps** Lifestyle apps have come strong in recent years. A Lifestyle app is one that accelerates or supports the individual facts that define your lifestyle. Some common Lifestyle mobile apps related to Fitness, Dating, Food, Music and Travel.

The beauty of these apps is that once they are a part of a user's lifestyle repertoire, they are likely there for good. These are the apps that people turn to on a daily basis to help them find the next new song, restaurant or destination.

Some examples of Lifestyle apps are

- Spotify
- Tripadvisor
- Uber

(ii) **Social Media Mobile Apps** Social media apps are some of the most popular types of mobile apps available. We build our social networks and most of us check in with them every day. Facebook alone reports over 1 billion active daily users. Social media apps have to be fun, fast and continually integrating the expanding features of the social networks they support. Today's society shares more about their day-to-day lives than ever before. For that reason, even apps that do not necessarily fall under the social media category may want to include social sharing functionality. Some common social media apps are

- Facebook
- Instagram
- Pinterest
- Snapchat

(iii) **Utility Mobile Apps** Utilities are the types of mobile apps that we may use most often without thinking about them as apps. Many of them come pre-installed on your device and serve a single function. Some common utility mobile apps are

- Reminders
- Calculator
- Flashlight
- Weather

(iv) **Games/Entertainment Mobile Apps** The gaming and entertainment category are huge and as such very competitive. Games are one of the more obvious mobile app categories and need little explanation. In the most successful games, both the frequency and length of play is high. Work to make your game as addictive as possible by offering incentives to users who come back every day or a certain number of days in a row.

Some common games apps are

- Angry Birds
- Clash of Clans
- Subway Surfer

(v) **Productivity Mobile Apps** While productivity may sound like one of the more boring types of mobile apps, it is incredibly popular category. These types of apps help their users accomplish a task quickly and efficiently.

Some common productivity apps are

- Docs
- Sheets
- Wallet/Pay
- Evernote
- Wunderlist

(vi) **News / Information Outlets** Mobile Apps News and information apps are pretty straightforward. They supply their users with the news and information they are looking for in an easy to understand layout that efficiently navigates them to the things they care about most.

Some common news apps are

- BuzzFeed
- SmartNews
- Google News & Weather
- Feedly
- Flipboard
- Yahoo News Digest
- Reddit
- LinkedIn Pulse

Chapter Practice

Objective Questions

• Multiple Choice Questions

1. Software commonly known as programs that consists of
(a) hardware
(b) input device
(c) instruction
(d) output device

Ans. (c) The computer software is a collection of programs and each program consists with set of instructions.

2. .... is a tool for graphic designers and non-designers to create visual communication.
(a) MS-Word
(b) Paintbrush
(c) MS-Excel
(d) DTP

Ans. (d) DTP is called as Desktop Publishing tools kit. It is used to design various kind of graphics and a work related to visual communication.

3. Identify, which is not a software?
(a) Payroll system
(b) Employee management
(c) CPU
(d) MS-Word

Ans. (c) From the given options, payroll system, employee management and MS-Word are the software but CPU is the type of hardware.

4. .... recognise input from keyboard and sends output to the display screen.
(a) Input device
(b) Operating system
(c) Printer
(d) Monitor

Ans. (b) Operating system is a system software, which acts as an interface between user and computer. Whenever user enters input it helps computer in recognising it.

5. Computer software can be categorised in two categories
(a) operating system and application
(b) compiler and translators
(c) system and application
(d) utility and application

Ans. (c) Computer software has two categories
System Software It is responsible for computer functioning.
Application Software It is a computer software designed to help the user to perform single or multiple tasks.

6. A computer software designed to help the user to perform single or .... tasks.
(a) two
(b) multiple
(c) exactly three
(d) only one

Ans. (b) Computer software is designed to help user for automation. With the help of software user can perform one or more than one task at the same time.

7. Which is the one is not an operating system?
(a) Windows 10
(b) DOS
(c) MAC OS
(d) Python

Ans. (d) Python is not an operating system. It is a programming language.

8. A program that can be used for managing salaries of the employees and staff is
(a) MS-Excel
(b) Payroll system
(c) Operating system
(d) CPU

Ans. (b) Payroll system is a software comes under the category if special purpose software. It is used to manage salaries of the employees in a company.

9. A .... is a system software that acts as an interface between the device and the user.
(a) MS-Excel
(b) device drivers
(c) operating system
(d) CPU

Ans. (b) The device drivers are the system software, which are responsible to make the interaction between a device and operating system.

10. Facebook comes under the category of which type of mobile app?
(a) Fitness
(b) Travel
(c) Social media
(d) Fooding

Ans. (c) There are various kind of mobile apps. Facebook is one of them. It is used to make a social presence of a person.

11. OS is a program that acts as an .... between the user and the hardware.
(a) software   (b) interface
(c) link   (d) device

Ans. (b) Operating system is a system software which acts as an interface between computer and a user.

12. An .... is an important component of a computer system, which controls and co-ordinates all other components of it.
(a) software   (b) hardware
(c) application   (d) operating system

Ans. (d) The operating system is responsible to make the coordination between all the components of the computer.

13. There are two categories of application software general purpose and .... purpose.
(a) system   (b) specific
(c) application   (d) device

Ans. (b) Application software are used by the user to perform a particular type of the task. There are two categories of application software- General purpose and Specific purpose.

14. Tally software is an example of .... purpose software.
(a) specific   (b) general   (c) system   (d) device

Ans. (a) Tally is used for the management of company accounts. It is an application software and comes under the category of specific work.

15. Calculator is a mobile app, which comes under the category of .... apps.
(a) food   (b) social
(c) utility   (d) mathematical

Ans. (c) Calculator is a mobile app, which comes under the category of utility apps.

16. Krishna has joined as computer operator in a company. His main task is to type letters and applications for the Boss. Help him which kind of software he requires in his computer?
(a) MS-Excel   (b) Paint brush
(c) MS-Word   (d) Tally

Ans. (c) The most suitable typing text software is MS- Word.

17. Nisha has purchased a new Laptop. Someone said to her you requires a system software to be installed to start working with it. Help her which software she requires first?
(a) MS-Word
(b) Device drivers
(c) Operating system
(d) Games

Ans. (c) The computer cannot work without having an operating system. It is system software helps computer to interact with a user.

• Case Based MCQs

Direction *Read the case and answer the following questions.*

18. Operating System (OS) is a program that acts as an interface between the user and the hardware. It is responsible to controls and co-ordinates all other components of the computer. It activates all devices and make them ready for work. It also performs all various functions to make all activities perfect and on time. The main functions of the OS includes

- It recognises input from keyboard and sends output to the display screen and make sure all the connected devices should work properly, called as device management.
- It makes sure that the programs running simultaneously do not interfere with each other, called as process management, this is also called as mutual exclusion .
- OS also responsible for security, ensuring that unauthorised users cannot access the system, etc . Operating System is of two types- Single user and multi-user. Examples of single user OS are – MS-DOS, Windows 95, etc. Some examples of multi-user OS are – Linux, Ubuntu, etc.

(i) Operating system activates .... and make them ready.
(a) software   (b) system
(c) devices   (d) buses

(ii) Which is a single user operating system?
(a) Linux   (b) Redhat
(c) DOS   (d) CentOS

(iii) Choose which is not a function of operating system?
(a) Device management   (b) Process management
(c) Employee management   (d) Memory management

(iv) As per the number of users the OS can be of .... types.
(a) one   (b) two
(c) three   (d) four

(v) .... is a function of OS in which OS recognise input from keyboard and sends output to the display screen and make sure all the connected devices are working properly.
(a) Process management   (b) Memory management
(c) Device management   (d) Employee management

Ans. (i) (*c*) It is a responsibility of OS to activate all the devices after power ON.

    (ii) (*c*) Disk Operating System (DOS) is a first single user operating system.

    (iii) (*c*) OS is a system software and its main functions are process management, device management and memory management. Employee management is an application program.

    (iv) (*b*) As per number of users OS is of two types – Single user and Multi-user.

    (v) (*c*) OS recognise input from keyboard and sends output to the display screen and make sure all the connected devices should work properly, called as device management.

19. Mobile applications which are popularly known as mobile apps, are software programs developed for mobile devices such as smartphones and tablets. Using these apps the mobile devices becomes miniature powerhouses for completion of various function and fun. Mobile phones generally come preloaded with various mobile apps provided free by the manufacturers or the mobile service providers. But there are various apps which are available only through device specific app stores. We can categorised mobile apps in six categories– Lifestyle apps (covers dating, food, fitness, etc.), Social media apps (facebook, twitter, etc.), Utility apps (reminder, weather, calendar, calculator, etc.), Gaming apps, Productivity apps and News apps. A mobile app is always has a smaller scope in comparison to the websites, means with less functionality.

  (i) Mobile apps are .... programs developed for mobile devices.

    (a) software   (b) hardware

    (c) device   (d) memory

  (ii) Mobile games apps if installed in mobile phone they make mobiles .... of fun.

    (a) versatile   (b) easy

    (c) handy   (d) powerhouse

  (iii) Some mobile apps comes with device, but there are various apps which are available only through device ....

    (a) company   (b) user

    (c) specific app stores   (d) app stores

  (iv) There are .... categories of mobile apps.

    (a) two   (b) four   (c) six   (d) five

  (v) Mobile apps has .... functionality in comparison to the websites.

    (a) more   (b) less   (c) maximum   (d) min

Ans. (i) (*a*) Mobile apps are software programs specially developed for mobile devices only.

    (ii) (*d*) Using these apps the mobile devices becomes miniature powerhouses for completion of various function and fun.

    (iii) (*c*) Some mobile apps comes with device, but there are various apps which are available only through device specific app stores. Mobile phones generally come preloaded with various mobile apps provided free by the manufacturers or the mobile service providers.

    (iv) (*c*) There are six types of mobile apps- Lifestyle apps, Social media apps, Utility apps, Gaming apps, Productivity apps and News apps.

    (v) (*b*) Mobile apps are very precise. These apps has less functionality in comparison to the main websites, so that it can consume less resource and battery.

PART 2
Subjective Questions

• Short Answer Type Questions

1. Write any three functions performed by operating system.

Ans. Functions performed by operating system are as follows

    (i) It recognises input from keyboard and sends output to the display screen.

    (ii) It makes sure that the programs running simultaneously do not interfere with each other.

    (iii) It manage the computer's resources, such as the Central Processing Unit (CPU), disk drives and printers.

2. What are the additional features provided by database management system?

Ans. Although, there are several features of database management system, but most popular are as follows

    (i) **Low Repetition and Redundancy** A DBMS reduces data repetition and redundancy by creating a single data repository accessible by multiple users and minimizing isolated files with repetition.

    (ii) **Muti-user Environment Support** A database management software features and supports a multi-user environment, allowing several users to access and work on data concurrently.

3. Write in short what is the purpose of device driver software?

Ans. A device driver is a system software that acts as an interface between the device and the user or an operating system. All computer accessories like : printer, scanner, web camera etc., have their own device driver software.

This software helps an operating system and other application software to communicate with a particular device for optimal use.

4. After installing an operating system, Nisha has connected her inkjet printer with laptop and trying to take the print. But, printer is not taking command. Can you rectify the problem?

Ans. Device driver for printer is not installed. Device driver is a system software required to be install to make an interface between operating system and device.

5. In how many category computer software can be categorised? Explain in brief, what is system software?

Ans. Computer software can be categorised into two major categories

(i) System Software (ii) Application Software

System Software All those programs which are used by a computer system either for its activation or internal resource management are called system software.
For example, software that would transfer the data/instructions from input devices to computer's memory will be a system software. It refers to the programs that control internal computer operations and makes best use of the hardware devices. System software can further be classified into various categories such as operating system, device drivers, language processors.

6. What is the use of application software? How many types of application software are available?

Ans. Application software are designed to help the user to perform single or multiple tasks. These software acts as a set of instructions, which directs the hardware to perform the specific functions.

For example, Accounting software, office suites, graphics software, media players etc.

Application software are categorised into two categories

(i) General purpose software
(ii) Specific purpose software

7. What is the use of word processing software? Name any two software applications used for word processing.

Ans. The word processing software is used to apply the basic editing and design and also helps in manipulating the text to your pages whereas the word processor, is a device that provides editing, input, formatting and output of the given text with some additional features. Microsoft Word and Google Docs are two of the most common word processing software applications.

8. In a XYZ company marketing manager is asked to give the total sales figure and future idea how sales can be increased area wise. Suggest which application software he can use to present data visually?

Ans. Manager can use presentation software for making data visualisation good. He can use MS-PowerPoint for making presentation. It is a general purpose application software, which allows user to present facts professionally with graphics and animations.

9. Explain, what is the use of inventory management system software.

Ans. Inventory Management System (IMS) is a specific purpose software, which can be used to attempt to balance inventory needs and requirement. This can ultimately help in minimising total cost and resulting from obtaining and holding an inventory. Some inventory management systems are Fishbowl, AdvancePro, etc.

10. List some most popular categories of accounting software.

Ans. Although, there are several types of accounting software categories but most popular are as follows

(i)   Accounts payable software
(ii) Bank reconciliation software
(iii) Budget management software

11. Software is not only the basic requirement of a computer system, it makes a computer more powerful and useful.
Computer systems divide software into two major classes.

(i) What is the meaning of the term software?

(ii) Name the two major classes of software.

Ans. (i) Software is a set of programs that tells the computer to perform a task.
(ii) Computer system divides software into two major categories
  (a) System software
  (b) Application software

12. Mr. X has recently installed a new operating system on his computer

(i) Describe the main functions of an operating system.

(ii) Name any two utility programs used by an operating system.

Ans. (i) Operating system monitors the performance of the system, enables software to communicate with hardware and application softwares to be loaded; gives prompts and error reports to the users.
(ii) Antivirus and compression tool.

13. What are mobile applications and how it is different from websites?

Ans. Mobile applications are light weight applications, designed especially for mobile devices. These apps are developed and designed in such a way, so that they can easily operate on small devices with small memory and limited battery.

These are different from websites because mobile apps generally have limited functionality and require limited resources.

• Long Answer Type Questions

14. Draw the proper classification chart of computer software.

Ans.

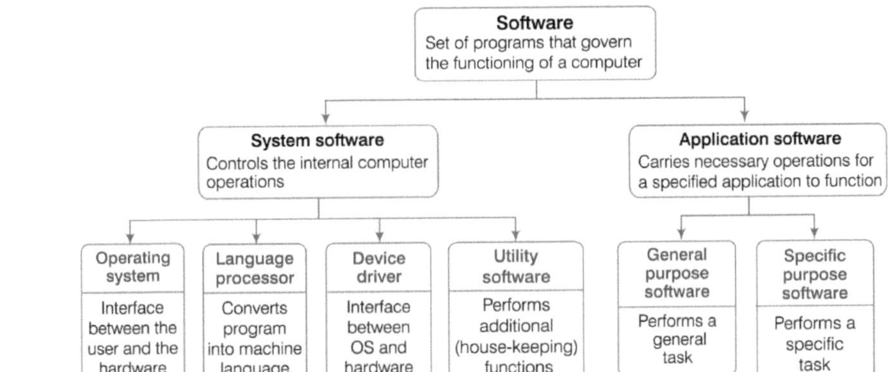

15. Define, what is the need of a language processors?

Ans. These are system software which are used to translate one language into another. As we know that computer is an electronic device and understands only binary language (0 and 1), but the user gives the instructions in either high level language or in low level language. Which means the computer cannot understand the instructions directly given by the user. The programs which are written by user in High level language such as : C, C++, Java or Python are called as source code. Every type of language has its own translator but we can categorise them in three categories

(i) **Compiler** It is a used to convert whole source code in a machine code in one step before execution. Languages in which compiler used are C, C++, Java, etc.

(ii) **Interpreter** It is used to convert each statement of the source program into machine code and executes it immediately before the conversion of the next statement. Languages in which interpreter used are Ruby, Python, etc.

(iii) **Assembler** It is a language processor which is used to translate the program written in low level language also called as an assembly language. It works in similar way as compiler.

16. What are specific purpose application software? Explain any two specific purpose softwares.

Ans. It is a type of software that is developed and designed to execute a specific task. *For example*, Hotel Management, Reservation System, Attendance System, Billing System etc. These softwares are called specific purpose application softwares because they target or address a very narrow solution to a problem. There can be variety of specific application softwares can be developed and also exist in the market. Any specific software may also be created in house and tailored to the specific needs of a user. The type of software developed to meet particular user specified requirements also falls into this category. Some of the specific purpose application softwares are as follows

(i) **Inventory Management System and Purchasing System** It is an software which is used to balance inventory needs and main need of the software to minimise the total cost, resulting from obtaining and holding an inventory.
For example, Fishbowl, AdvancePro etc.

(ii) **Payroll Management System** It is used by all modern organisations to encompass every employee of the organisation, who receives regular wages or other compensation. All different payment methods are calculated by the payroll software and the appropriate pay checks are issued. This software can also be used for printing or E-mailing the salary slip of employees.
For example, Namely, UltiPro etc.

17. Reena got an assignment on the topic word processing software. Help her to solve the assignment.
(i) What is word processing software?
(ii) Which type of software is word processor?
(iii) Give some examples equivalent to type of word processing software.
(iv) Give some examples of word processing program.

Ans. (i) Word processing software is an application software that helps to create text based documents. It also processes paragraphs, pages and entire papers.
(ii) General purpose application software is word processor.
(iii) Electronic spreadsheets, database management systems, desktop publishing software, graphics, multimedia and presentation applications.
(iv) Microsoft Word, WordPerfect (Windows only), AppleWorks (Mac only) and OpenOffice.org Writer.

18. Below is the list of various types of application softwares.

A. Database

B. Desktop publishing

C. Drawing

D. Word processing

E. Spreadsheet

Which one would be the most suitable to use for each of the following tasks?

(i) Rotation of shapes

(ii) Typing in text for a novel

(iii) Using frames to position text and graphics on a page

(iv) Replication of cells

(v) Carrying out a complex search on two or more criteria

Ans. (i) C. Drawing

(ii) D. Word processing

(iii) B. Desktop publishing

(iv) E. Spreadsheet

(v) A. Database

19. What are the six categories of mobile applications? Explain any three of them.

Ans. Mobile applications (also known as mobile apps) are software programs developed for mobile devices such as smartphones and tablets.

Six types of mobile apps are as follows

(i) Lifestyle

(ii) Social media

(iii) Utility

(iv) Games

(v) Productivity

(vi) News

(i) **Lifestyle Mobile Apps** Lifestyle apps have come on strong in recent years. A Lifestyle app is one that accelerates or supports the individual facts that define your lifestyle. Some common Lifestyle mobile apps are Fitness, Dating, Food, Music and Travel.

The beauty of these apps is that once they are a part of a user's lifestyle repertoire, they are likely there for good. These are the apps that people turn to on a daily basis to help them find the next new song, restaurant or destination.

Some examples of Lifestyle apps are

- Spotify
- Tripadvisor
- Uber

(ii) **Social Media Mobile Apps** Social media apps are some of the most popular types of mobile apps available. We build our social networks and most of us check in with them every day. Facebook alone reports over 1 billion active daily users. Social media apps have to be fun, fast and continually integrating the expanding features of the social networks they support. Today's society shares more about their day-to-day lives than ever before. For that reason, even apps that don't necessarily fall under the social media category may want to include social sharing functionality.

Some common social media apps are

- Facebook
- Instagram
- Pinterest
- Snapchat

(iii) **Utility Mobile Apps** Utilities are the types of mobile apps that we may use most often without thinking about them as apps. Many of them come pre-installed on your device and serve a single function.

Some common utility mobile apps are

- Reminders
- Calculator
- Flashlight
- Weather

Chapter Test

Multiple Choice Questions

1. Which of the refers to the set of instructions?
(a) Software   (b) Program   (c) Application   (d) Utility

2. Special type of system software that helps in compression of file is called as .... software.
(a) application   (b) system   (c) utility   (d) specific

3. A .... is a piece of software specifically designed to installed on handheld smart devices.
(a) smart app   (b) mobile app   (c) application app   (d) software app

4. Command can be given by only .... in CUI OS.
(a) sending   (b) typing   (c) icons   (d) pointing

5. As per the interface OS can be of two types CUI and ....
(a) GUI   (b) PUI   (c) DUI   (d) TUI

6. Teacher asked Ram to identify OS of his laptop as per the given user interface. Windows 10 OS is installed in Ram's laptop. Ram said it is a .... operating system.
(a) CUI   (b) single user   (c) GUI   (d) DUI

7. Neha wants to set a reminder in her mobile. She is looking for it but not finding it. There are some categories of apps given in her mobile – Social apps, Lifestyle apps and Utility apps. Help Neha to find the reminder app in her mobile.
(a) Lifestyle   (b) Utility   (c) Social   (d) It is not in mobile

Short Answer Type Questions

8. Niti is a student of Class 9th. She has to complete her assignment of computer application subject. In her assignment, she got a question like "What is the difference between computer utility softwares and mobile utility apps?". In which she is confuse what to write ? Help her in solving this question.

9. Name the category of the following softwares
(i) Railway reservation system
(ii) MS- Word
(iii) Inventory management
(iv) Compiler
(v) Winzip file compression

10. Differentiate between compiler and interpreter.

11. Explain the following terms.
(i) Assembler
(ii) Presentation software

Long Answer Type Questions

12. Differentiate between system software and application software.

13. What is operating system? How can we categorise, the operating system on the basis of interface? Give one example of each.

14. What are the functions of utility software. Explain in brief.

Answers

Multiple Choice Questions

1. (b)   *2. (c)*   *3. (b)*   *4. (b)*   *5. (a)*   *6. (c)*   *7. (b)*

For Detailed Solutions
Scan the code

CHAPTER 04

Computer Network

In this Chapter...

- Needs for Computer Network
- Types of Computer Network
- Communication Channels
- Cloud Computing
- Multimedia

A network can be defined as a group of devices connected to each other, i.e. a network allows the exchange data through connected devices. Thus, a network is a series of nodes interconnected by communication paths.

Network can be interconnected with other networks and also contain sub-networks. Networking is a process of exchanging the information and ideas among individuals or groups that share a common interest, i.e. the process of creating a network is called networking.

A computer network is formed with the intention of sharing files, resources (e.g. printers, hard disks etc.) and softwares (e.g. MS-Word). The best computer network is the Internet.

Needs for Computer Network

There are some needs and benefits of a computer network

(i) **File and Data Sharing** At a time, file sharing consisted mostly of saving documents to floppy disks that could be physically transferred to other computers by hand. With networking, files can be shared instantaneously across the network, whether with one user or with hundred users. e.g. employees across departments can collaborate on documents, exchange background material etc.

(ii) **Resource Sharing** Computer networking also allows the sharing of network resources, such as printers, scanners, dedicated servers, backup systems, input devices and Internet connections. By sharing resources, unique equipment like scanners, printers etc., can be made available to all network users simultaneously without being relocated, eliminating the need for expensive redundancies.

(iii) **Data Protection and Redundancy** Computer networking allows users to distribute copies of important information across multiple locations, ensuring essential information is not lost with the failure of any one computer in the network. By utilising central backup systems both on-site and off-site, unique documents and data can be gathered automatically from every computer in the network and securely backed up in case of physical computer damage or accidental deletion.

(iv) **Ease of Administration** Instead of individually upgrading each computer in an organisation, a network administrator can initiate an upgrade from a server and automatically duplicate the upgrade throughout the network. Simultaneously, allowing everyone in the company to maintain uniform software, resources and procedures.

(v) **User Communication** Computer networking also allows organisations to maintain complex communication systems. It also allows users to communicate using E-mail, newsgroups, video conferencing etc.

(vi) **Distributed Computing Power** In computer networks, we can distribute tasks across multiple computers throughout the network, by breaking complex problems into hundreds or thousands of smaller operations, which are then parcelled out to individual computers. Each computer in the network performs its operations on its own portion of the larger problem and return its result. Then, all these results are gathered in such a form that impact as the solution of the complex problem and finally are used for the further task.

(vii) **Network Gaming** A lot of network games are available, which allow multi-users to play from different locations. It is a type of online game, i.e. played through social networks.

Types of Computer Network

Based on the geographical area covered and data transfer rate, computer networks are broadly categorised as

1. Local Area Network (LAN)

A local area network is a computer network covering a small geographical area like a home, office or small group of buildings such as within a school. It is suitable for small sites. Computers connected to a LAN can share information and peripheral equipment. LAN are widely used to allow resources to be shared between personal computers or workstations. This kind of network can be extended upto 1 km. Data transfer in LAN is quite and usually varies from 10 Mbps to 1000 Mbps.

2. Metropolitan Area Network (MAN)

A metropolitan area network is a large computer network that usually spans a city or a large campus. A MAN usually interconnects a number of local area networks. So that, resources can be shared LAN to LAN as well as device to device. A MAN can be wholly owned and operated by a private company. This kind of network can be extended upto 30-40 km.

3. Wide Area Network (WAN)

A wide area network is a computer network that covers a broad area such as any network whose communication links across metropolitan, regional, national or international boundaries.

WANs are used to connect LANs and other types of network together, so that users and computers in one location can communicate with users and computers in other locations. Mainly WAN is used by business, organisation and governments or by individuals. The biggest example of WAN is Internet.

Differences between LAN, MAN and WAN

Basis	LAN	MAN	WAN
Geographical Area	Generally within a building	Within a city	Across the continents
Cost	Less expensive	More than LAN but less than WAN	More than MAN
Ownership	Private	Private or Public	Shared across the world
Example	Network within school	Cable TV network within a city	Internet

4. Personal Area Network (PAN)

A personal area network is a computer network used for communication among computer and different information technological devices close to one person. Some examples of devices that are used in a PAN are personal computers, printers, fax machines, telephones, PDAs, scanners and even video game consoles. A PAN may include wired and wireless devices. The reach of a PAN typically extends to 10 metres. A wired PAN is usually constructed with USB and Firewire connections while technologies such as Bluetooth and infrared communication typically form a wireless PAN.

Communication Channels

Communication channel or transmission media is the link between two computers in which data is transferred between them. Thus, transmission media is a pathway that carries the information from sender to receiver. These are categorised into two types

1. Wired or Guided media
2. Wireless or Unguided media

Guided media are generally used for establishing LAN and MAN while unguided media are used for WAN.

1. Wired or Guided Media

In this type of communication channel, as the name suggests, wires or cables are used for connecting two or more computers to transmit data. It is also called guided media because of the use of cables, signals are guided through a specific path. Since, data signals are bounded, it is also called **bounded media**.

Various types of guided media are as follows

(i) Twisted Pair Cable

This is the most common type of communication channel. It consists of two insulated wires twisted around each other and uses copper as a conductor.

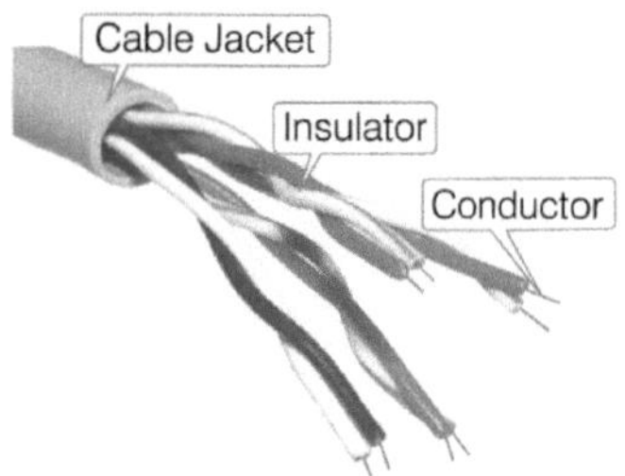

Twisted pair cable

This property of twisted pair cable provides protection against crosstalk and noise. There are two types of twisted pair cables as follows

- **Shielded Twisted Pair (STP) Cable** This version of twisted pair was created by IBM. It consists of a metal shield covering each pair of insulated wires.
- **Unshielded Twisted Pair (UTP) Cable** It is the copper media, inherited from telephony, which is being used for increasing higher data rates. It is used in ethernet networks and in telephone systems.

Advantages The advantages of twisted pair cable are as follows

- It has very light weight.
- Its cost is very low.
- It is easy to install and maintain.
- It supports analog as well as digital transmission.
- It is physically flexible.

Disadvantages The disadvantages of twisted pair cable are as follows

- Because of high attenuation, signals cannot be transported over a long distance without using repeaters.
- Data rates supported are 1 Mbps to 10 Mbps.
- Its low bandwidth capabilities make it unsuitable for broadband applications.
- Not a secure medium, it can be easily tapped.

(ii) Co-axial Cable

It contains two conductors that are parallel to each other, i.e. first is the **inner conductor** or **core conductor** made of solid copper and the second is the **outer conductor**, which serves as a shield against noise. An insulating plastic is placed between the two conductors and this whole setup is covered with a plastic jacket.

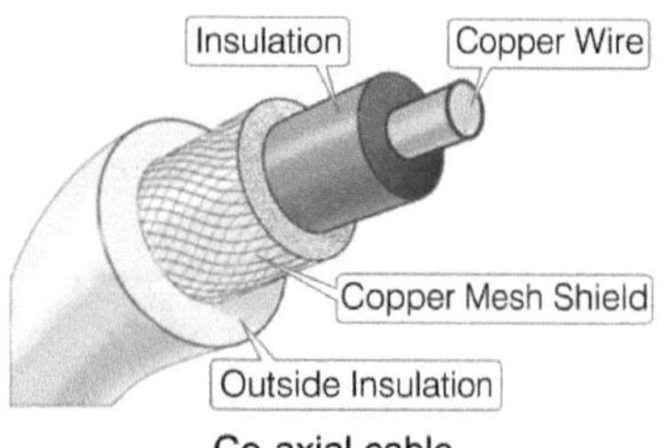

Co-axial cable

Advantages The advantages of co-axial cable are as follows

- Transmission quality of co-axial cable is better than twisted pair cable. It can transmit several channels simultaneously, so these channels are used in cable TV network.
- It can be used for broadband transmission.
- It offers higher bandwidth upto 450 Mbps.

Disadvantages The disadvantages of co-axial cable are as follows

- More costly than twisted pair cable.
- These are not compatible with twisted pair cable.
- It is difficult to install.
- Failure of the single cable results to fail the entire network.

(iii) Optical Fibre

These are similar to co-axial cable. It consists of thin strands made up of glass or glass like material, which are capable of carrying light signals from a source at one end to another end.

There are three main parts in optical fibre

- **Core** It is the section through which the data travels in the form of light. Typically, core has a diameter of 62.5 microns.
- **Cladding** It is the covering part of core. Its function is to reflect back the light into the core, as it is a denser medium. Typically, cladding has a diameter of 125 microns.
- **Protective Coating** It is the outer cover of cladding for the protection of optical fibre from damage and moisture. It is also called **jacket** or **sheath**. Typically, coating has a diameter of 250 microns.

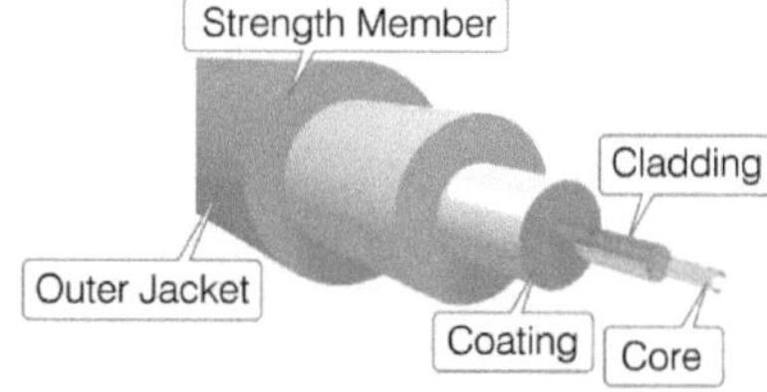

Optical fibre

Advantages The advantages of optical fibre are as follows

- These are highly suitable for harsh industrial environment. These are immune to noise caused by electrical and magnetic fields.
- It can support dramatically higher bandwidths (and hence data rates) than either twisted pair or co-axial cable.
- Less signal attenuation.
- These are much lighter than copper cables.

Disadvantages The disadvantages of optical fibre are as follows

- These are very difficult to install and maintain.
- They require more protection around the cable than copper cables.

- Propagation of light is uni-directional. For bi-directional communication, two fibres are needed. These are relatively more expensive than other guided media.

(iv) Ethernet Cable

An ethernet cable is one of the most popular form of network cables used on wired networks. It connects devices on LAN such as PCs, routers and switches. A crossover cable is a special type of ethernet cable specially designed for connecting two computers to each other.

By contrast, most ethernet cables are designed to connect one computer to a router or a switch. A single ethernet cable can extend only limited distances due to their electrical transmission characteristics. RJ-45 is the most commonly used ethernet cable.

Advantages The advantages of ethernet cable are as follows

- It gives fast, secured, reliable transmission across them and external disturbances are very less.
- You can transfer any large data between two or more PC's which are locally connected through ethernet.
- These are robust to noise, thus external disturbances are very less.

Disadvantages The disadvantages of ethernet cable are as follows

- As the load on ethernet increases, number of collision increases, therefore efficiency decreases.
- It offers non-deterministic service, so it is not suitable for real-time application.
- Higher costs for provisioning in existing building.

2. Wireless or Unguided Media

This type of communication channel uses waves to transfer data, i.e. no cables are needed to guide the signals. Hence, this is called unguided media. In this, signals are not bounded to any cabling system, therefore this is also called **unbounded media**.

These can be categorised are as follows

(i) Long Distance Wireless Media

It supports communication over long distances, i.e. upto thousands of kilometres. Long distance wireless media are as follows

(a) **Microwave** In this type of transmission, microwaves are used as an alternative of co-axial cable to transmit data over long distances. It is also known as 802.16. Microwave transmission supports line-of-sight transmission, i.e. signals travel in a straight line.

   Advantages The advantages of microwave are as follows

- It provides multi-channel transmissions.
- Communication is possible even in difficult rain.
- Requires less number of amplifiers and repeaters.

   Disadvantages The disadvantages of microwave are as follows

- Insecure communication, as the tapping of microwave is easy.
- It is affected by the weather conditions such as rain, thunder, storm etc.
- Cost of maintenance, implementation and design is high.

(b) **Radiowave** When two computers communicate by using radio frequencies, then such type of communication is known as radiowave transmission. Radio waves are omni-directional, i.e. they travel in all directions. It can be classified by frequency and wavelength. When the frequency is higher than 3GHz, it is named as microwave.

   Advantages The advantages of radiowave are as follows

- They provide enhanced audio volume and clarity.
- They improve accuracy and allow data transmission over long distances. It is cheaper technology.

   Disadvantages The disadvantages of radiowave are as follows

- Physical interrupt such as mountains and buildings can prevent or interfere with transmission.
- Any correctly tuned receiver within the range can pick the radiowave signals.
- It is not secured communication medium.

(c) **Satellite** Satellites are an essential part of telecommunication systems. They carry a large amount of data in addition to TV signals. When the data is transmitted using satellite, then it is said to be satellite communication. A satellite communication consists of an earth station and a satellite at a stationary orbit, which is about 22300 miles above the earth's surface.

A satellite communication is a space station that receives microwave signals from an earth-based station, amplifies the signals and broadcasts the signals back over a wide area to any number of earth-based stations.

   Advantages The advantages of satellite are as follows

- It covers a very vast area.
- The wired communication is almost impossible and too costly to use across the continents, whereas the satellite communication proves to be the best.
- It is very useful in television transmission.
- Higher bandwidths are available for use.

   Disadvantages The disadvantages of satellite are as follows

- Launching satellite into orbit is costly.
- There is atmospheric loss of transmitted signals.
- Interference and propagation delay.

(ii) Short Distance Wireless Media

It supports communication over a small distance, generally few miles to a few kilometres. The following are the types covered under short distance wireless media

(a) **Infrared** This type of wireless media uses infrared light for the transmission of data. Infrared light lies between the visible and microwave portions of the electromagnetic spectrum and is not visible to the human eyes.

Infrared is used for indoor wireless LANs and also use line-of-sight propagation. It cannot pass through solid objects like walls and offers large bandwidth for use. We cannot use infrared waves outside a building because the sun's rays contain infrared waves that can interfere with the communication.

Advantages The advantages of infrared are as follows

- It consumes less power.
- Circuitry cost is less.
- It includes simple circuitry.
- It can be activated with almost any device.

Disadvantages The disadvantages of infrared are as follows

- Line-of-sight is needed for communication.
- Can be blocked by common materials like walls, people, plants etc. This can be used only in enclosed rooms.

(b) **Bluetooth** It is a simple, secure and universal wireless communication technology. It refers to a wireless technology that creates small wireless networks, called Personal Area Network (PAN) between PCs and peripheral devices.

The bluetooth wireless technology enables you to establish a wireless communication between any two bluetooth devices, such as mobile phones, laptops, cameras or modem stations without any cables. The data transfer rate over the bluetooth varies from 723 Kbps to 1 Mbps in a short range. The standard specification mandates a minimum range of 100 m (328 feet).

Advantages The advantages of bluetooth are as follows

- It can share data without any wire.
- It consumes low power and low processing.
- It is free to use, if the device is bluetooth enabled.
- Connecting two different devices using bluetooth is very convenient.

Disadvantages The disadvantages of bluetooth are as follows

- Only short range communication is possible.

- Connection can be lost under certain conditions.
- It can be easily hacked.

(c) **Wi-Fi** Wi-Fi stands for Wireless Fidelity, has a range of about 100 m and allows for faster rate between 10-54 Mbps. Wi-Fi services have been introduced for providing high speed Internet access at convenient public locations such as Airports, Universities etc. Wi-Fi is another name for wireless LAN or WLAN. Home and business networks (private) and public hotspots use it to connect computers and other wireless devices to each other with Internet. Computers and other devices connect to a Wi-Fi network via a wireless router or access point. For Wi-Fi to work, we need

- A broadband Internet connection
- A wireless router
- A laptop or PC having wireless Internet card or external wireless adapter.

Advantages The advantages of Wi-Fi are as follows

- It can be used while moving within the signal range.
- Network can be created where you cannot lay cable network. It is a wireless connection that can merge together multiple devices.

Disadvantages The disadvantages of Wi-Fi are as follows

- It is more costly than wired network.
- Radiation generated by Wi-Fi can effect human health.
- Power consumption is fairly high.

Differences between Wired and Wireless Communication Channels

Wired Communication Channel	Wireless Communication Channel
It is more secure.	More security measures need to be considered for providing security.
If is faster than wireless communication.	It is slower than wired communication.
Technically less difficult to set-up.	Technically more difficult to set-up.
More expensive for longer distances.	Less expensive for long distances.
User device cannot be moved.	User device can be moved easily within the wireless range.

Cloud Computing

It provides computing and storage capacity services to heterogeneous community of end recipients.

The name comes from the use of clouds as an abstraction for the complex infrastructure, it contains in system diagrams.

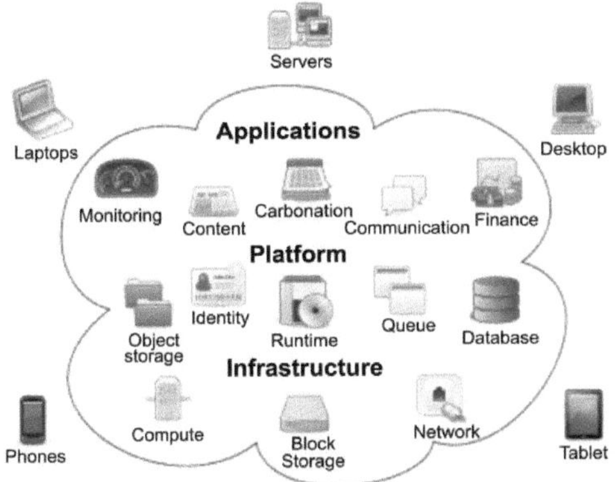

Cloud computing

It entrusts services with a user's data, software and computation over a network. It has considerable overlap with Software as a Service (SaaS).

Essential Characteristics of Cloud Computing

- **On Demand Self Services** Computer services such as E-mail, applications, network or server service can be provided without requiring human interaction with each service provider.

- **Broad Network Access** Cloud capabilities are available over the network and accessed through standard mechanisms that promote use by heterogeneous thin or thick client platforms such as mobile phones, laptops and PDAs.

- **Resource Pooling** The provider's computing resources are pooled together to serve multiple consumers using multiple-tenant model with different physical and virtual resources dynamically assigned and reassigned according to consumer demand.

- **Rapid Elasticity** Cloud services can be rapidly and elastically provisioned, in some cases automatically, to quickly scale out and rapidly released to quickly scale in.

- **Measured Service** Cloud computing resource usage can be measured, controlled and reported providing transparency for both the provider and consumer of the utilised service.

- **Multi Tenacity** It refers to the need for policy-driven enforcement, segmentation, isolation, governance, service levels and chargeback/billing models for different consumer constituencies.

Applications of Cloud Computing

The applications of cloud computing are practically limitless. With the right middleware, a cloud computing system could execute all the programs a normal computer could run. Potentially, everything from generic word processing software to customised computer programs designed for a specific company could work on a cloud computing system.

The applications of cloud computing are as follows

- Clients would be able to access their applications and data from anywhere at any time.

- It could bring hardware costs down. You would not need a large hard drive because you would store all your information on a remote computer.

- Corporations that rely on computers have to make sure they have the right software in place to achieve goals. Cloud computing systems give these organisations company-wide access to computer applications. The companies do not have to buy a set of softwares or software licenses for every employee. Instead, the company could pay a metered fee to a cloud computing company.

- Servers and digital storage devices take up space. Some companies rent physical space to store servers and databases because they don't have it available on site. Cloud computing gives these companies the option of need for physical space on the front end.

- Corporations might save money on IT support. Streamlined hardware would, in theory, have fewer problems than a network of heterogeneous machines and operating systems.

Types of Cloud Deployments

There are three cloud deployment models : public, private and hybrid. Each deployment model is defined according to where the infrastructure for the environment is located.

(i) Public Cloud

Public clouds are owned and operated by a third party cloud service provider, which deliver their computing resources like servers and storage over the Internet. With a public cloud, all hardware, software and other supporting infrastructure is owned and managed by the cloud provider. You access these services and manage your account using a web browser.

(ii) Private Cloud

A private cloud refers to cloud computing resources used exclusively by a single business or organisation. A private cloud can be physically located on the company's on-site data center. Some companies also pay third party service providers to host their private cloud. A private cloud is one in which the services and infrastructure are maintained on a private network.

(iii) Hybrid Cloud

Hybrid clouds combine public and private clouds. They bound together by technology that allows data and applications to be shared between them. By allowing data and applications to move between private and public clouds, hybrid cloud gives businesses greater flexibility and more deployment options.

Multimedia

Any combination of text, graphic art, sound, video and animation to any individual by computer or other electronic means is known as multimedia. Multimedia stimulates the eyes, ears and brain of the person. Multimedia may be any of the following

(i) Text and sound.

(ii) Text, sound and still or animated graphic images.

(iii) Text, sound and video images.

(iv) Video and sound.

(v) Multiple display areas, images or presentations, presented concurrently.

Multimedia is a very effective presentation tool. Studies indicate that, if a person is stimulated with audio then assumption rate would be upto 20 per cent, with audio-visual. It would be upto 30 per cent with interactive multimedia presentations and assumption rate can be increased upto 60 per cent. Multimedia can be broadly divided into following two categories

- **Linear multimedia** This type of content generally progresses without any navigational control for the viewer. e.g. PowerPoint presentation, anime episode.

- **Non-linear multimedia** This type of content uses interactivity to control progress. e.g. a video game, hypermedia.

Components of Multimedia

Various components of multimedia are as follows

(i) Text

Text content is by far the most common media type in computing applications. Most multimedia systems use a combination of text and other media to deliver functionality. Text in multimedia systems can express specific information, or it can act as reinforcement for information contained in other media items. Multimedia provide many text based languages like XML, HTML and JavaScript.

Generally, used text formats are TXT, DOC etc. e.g. when web pages include image elements, they can also include a short amount of text for the user's browser to include as an alternative. In this case, the digital image item is not available.

(ii) Images

Digital image files appear in many multimedia applications. Digital photographs can display application content or can alternatively form part of a user interface.

Interactive elements such as buttons, often use custom images created by the designers and developers involved in an application.

Digital image files use a variety of formats and file extensions. Among them, most common are JPEGs and PNGs. Both of these often appear on websites, as the formats allow developers to minimise the file size while maximising on picture quality. Graphic design software programs such as photoshop and Paint allow developers to create complex visual effects with digital images.

(iii) Audio

Audio files and streams play a major role in some multimedia systems. Audio files appear as a part of application content to aid interaction. Audio formats include MP3, WMA, WAV, MIDI and RealAudio. When developers include audio within a website, they will generally use a compressed format to minimise download times. Web services can also stream audio, so that users can begin playback before the entire file is downloaded.

(iv) Video

Digital video appears in many multimedia applications, particularly on the web. As with audio, websites can stream digital video to increase the speed and availability of playback. Common digital video formats include flash, MPEG, AVI, WMV and Quick Time. Most digital video requires use of browser plug-in to play the video.

(v) Animation

Animated components are common within both web and desktop multimedia applications. It can also include interactive effects, allowing users to engage with the animation action using their mouse and keyboard. The most common tool for creating animations on the web is adobe flash, which also facilitates desktop applications. Animation formats include SWF, FXG, WNF etc.

Chapter Practice

Objective Questions

• Multiple Choice Questions

1. Several computers linked to a server to share programs and storage space is form ....
(a) Library   (b) Network
(c) Group   (d) System

Ans. (b) Network is a collection of computers connected to share common resources where several computers linked to server for sharing program or other resources.

2. .... is a pathway that carries the information from sender to receiver.
(a) Computer
(b) Transmission media
(c) CPU
(d) Network

Ans. (b) Transmission media is a pathway that carries the information from sender to receiver. Data is transmitted through the electromagnetic signals.

3. A .... network can be established inside a building using cables.
(a) LAN   (b) MAN
(c) WAN   (d) Internet

Ans. (a) LAN is called as local area network. It is a network which is established for making network inside a building or a lab.

4. Full form of WAN is
(a) Wide Area Net
(b) Wise Area Network
(c) Wide Area Network
(d) Wise Area Net

Ans. (c) The WAN is called as Wide Area Network. It is also called an Internet.

5. Which wireless media is used for short distance?
(a) Cable   (b) Infrared
(c) Fibre optics   (d) Phone

Ans. (b) Infrared is called as short distance wireless media. It uses infrared light for data transmission.

6. .... can be used to create a wireless PAN.
(a) Cable   (b) Bluetooth
(c) Internet   (d) LAN

Ans. (b) Bluetooth used for wireless network connections such as PAN to connect personal peripheral devices for data transmission.

7. Range of Wi-Fi is about
(a) 100 m   (b) 110 m
(c) 200 m   (c) 1000 m

Ans. (a) Wi-Fi is called as wireless fidelity network technology. Its range is about 100 m.

8. Co-axial cable contains .... conductors.
(a) one   (b) two
(c) three   (d) None of these

Ans. (b) The co-axial cable used a communication channel for LAN for data transmission. It contains two conductors – inner and outer.

9. Which is not an essential characteristics of cloud computing?
(a) Resource pooling
(b) Elasticity
(c) Pumpicity
(d) Measured service

Ans. (c) There are five essential characteristics of cloud computing- resource pooling, measured services, broad network access, elasticity and multi tenancy.

10. Which type of cloud can be physically located on the company's on-site data centre?
(a) Private cloud
(b) Public cloud
(c) Hybrid cloud
(d) None of the above

Ans. (a) A private cloud is generally physically located on company's site.

Ans. (c) Chat is a real-time application used in mobile devices.

11. There are two types of communication channel wired and ....
(a) Wi-Fi   (b) wireless
(c) wireprone   (d) private

Ans. (b) There are two types of communication channel used for networking- wired and wireless.

12. The data transfer rate over the Bluetooth varies from 723 .... to 1 Mbps.

(a) Mbps   (b) bps   (c) Kbps   (d) Gbps

Ans. (c) Bluetooth is a wireless short distance technology to share data among personal devices. The general range of data transfer is 723 Kbps to 1 Mbps.

13. .... is the most commonly used Ethernet cable.

(a) RJ-45   (b) RF-45   (c) RF-48   (d) RJ-48

Ans. (a) The most commonly used Ethernet cable is RJ-45.

14. Multimedia stimulates the eyes, ... and brain of the person.

(a) hand   (b) nose   (c) ears   (d) leg

Ans. (c) Multimedia is a combinations of Text, graphics, sound, videos etc. It stimulates the eyes, ears and brain of the person

15. Harish is right now working from home. He requires a good internet connection speed for doing his work. Suggest, what kind of connection he should buy?

(a) Internet   (b) Wi-Fi
(c) Bluetooth   (d) Infrared

Ans. (b) Wi-Fi is a short distance wireless network. Best to access the Internet using mobile devices.

16. Niti has started a new company. She do not want to invest much amount in IT infrastructure such as – processor, software etc. Suggest through which technology she can save cost?

(a) Mobile   (b) Internet
(c) Cloud computing   (d) Wi-Fi

Ans. (c) Cloud computing is a huge resource pool which can be access anywhere anytime.

• Case Based MCQs

Direction *Read the case and answer the following questions.*

17. When group of computers are connected together for sharing of resources, then it is called as computer network. There are various benefits of using computer networks such as – file and data sharing, device sharing, centralised administration of any work, distribution of work, etc. The device sharing also called as resource sharing is the major objective of computer networking. Costly devices such as printers, scanners, dedicated servers, backup systems, input devices and Internet connections can be easily shared with networking among all available network users simultaneously without being relocated. It also eliminating the need for expensive redundancies. Apart from resource sharing networking can protect data from hacking and loss by keeping data at multiple places. Keeping data at multiple places can ensure no loss of data by any accidental deletion or any other situation.

(i) Group of computers connected together for .... of costly devices called as computer network.

(a) creating   (b) sharing
(c) adding   (d) None of these

(ii) Resource sharing is also called as .... sharing.

(a) human   (b) cable   (c) device   (d) tab

(iii) The resources can be sharing with only those users who are .... to network right now.

(a) shared   (b) connected
(c) sleeping   (d) not available

(iv) Data .... can be done, if user keep copies of data at multiple places.

(a) loss   (b) connection
(c) backup   (d) print

(v) The .... connections can be easily shared with computer network among all available network users at the same time without being relocated.

(a) cable   (b) Internet
(c) network   (d) data

Ans. (i) (a) Group of computers are connected to share costly resources or devices then it is called as computer network.

(ii) (c) Resources in terms of computer network are also called as devices.

(iii) (b) The resources of the network can be shared with only connected users.

(iv) (c) Data backup can be achieved, if data is kept at multiple places.

(v) (b) The Internet connection can be easily shared in LAN very easily among all available users.

18. When large number of resources are pool together and can be shared among multiple users on demand in flexi manner anywhere any time can be referred as a cloud environment. There are five essential characteristics of the cloud computing – elasticity, resource pool, network access, measure services and multi tenancy.

There are three deployment models of the cloud – private, public and hybrid. There are limitless applications of the cloud computing. With the right middleware, a cloud computing system could execute all the programs a normal computer could run. The main benefits of cloud computing included data access anywhere any time. Less cost investment in infrastructure and maintenance is required. A company can hire resources from cloud on demand basis and pay as per the utilisation of the resource.

(i) The large number of .... are pooled in cloud.
  (a) resources   (b) time
  (c) task   (d) None of these

(ii) Which is a characteristic of the cloud computing?
  (a) Public   (b) Topacity
  (c) Middleware   (d) Elasticity

(iii) Which is not a deployment model of cloud?
  (a) Private   (b) Hybrid
  (c) Local   (d) Public

(iv) The main benefit of cloud computing is access data .... anytime.
  (a) temporary   (b) anywhere
  (c) onsite   (d) None of these

(v) We can save the cost of .... by using cloud computing technology.
  (a) data   (b) mobile
  (c) infrastructure   (d) print

Ans. (i) (*a*) The cloud is a pool of large number of resources.

(ii) (*d*) The elasticity is a characteristic of the cloud computing among five essential characteristics.

(iii) (*c*) There are three deployment models of the cloud computing- Private, public and hybrid.

(iv) (*b*) Using cloud computing data can be accessed anywhere anytime.

(v) (*c*) Company can save the cost in infrastructure by using the cloud computing technology.

PART 2
Subjective Questions

• Short Answer Type Questions

1. What is full form of Wi-Fi? Why it is required?

Ans. Wi-Fi is called as Wireless Fidelity network. It is a wireless technology used to connect computers, tablets, smartphones and other devices to the Internet.

2. What are the types of twisted pair cable?

Ans. There are two types of twisted pair cable, which are as follows

(i) **Shielded Twisted Pair (STP) Cable** This type of twisted pair was created by a company IBM. It consists of a metal shield which covers each pair of insulated wires.

(ii) **Unshielded Twisted Pair (UTP) Cable** It is the copper media, which is inherited from telephony. It is used in Ethernet networks and in telephone systems.

3. What are the three parts of optical fibre cable?

Ans. The three parts of optical fibre cable are as follows

(i) **Core** It is a first section through which the data travels in the form of light. Its diameter is approximately follows 62.5 microns.

(ii) **Cladding** It is a covering part of the core. Its main function is to reflect back the light into the core.

(iii) **Protective Coating** It is a outer most cover, which is after cladding. Its work to protect optical fibre from damage and moisture.

4. Which type of signals are received by the satellite space station from earth station?

Ans. In a satellite communication there is a space station that receives the microwave signals from an earth-based station. It amplifies the signals and then broadcasts signals back over a wide area to any number of earth-based stations.

5. Differentiate among LAN, MAN and WAN.

Ans. Differences among LAN, MAN and WAN are as follows

Basis	LAN	MAN	WAN
Geographical Area	Generally within a building	Within a city	Across the continents
Cost	Less expensive	More than LAN but less than WAN	More than MAN
Ownership	Private	Private or public	Shared across the world
Example	Network within school	Cable TV network within a city	Internet

6. What are the requirements for Wi-Fi to work?

Ans. There are various requirements for Wi-Fi to work

(i) A broadband Internet connection.

(ii) A wireless router.

(iii) A laptop or PC having wireless Internet card or external wireless adapter.

7. Explain the distributed computing power can be achieved using networking.

Ans. In computer networks, we can distribute tasks across multiple computers throughout the network, by breaking complex problems into hundreds or thousands of smaller operations, which are then parcelled out to individual computers. Each computer in the network performs its operations on its own portion of the larger problem and return its result. Then, all these results are gathered in such a form that impact as the solution of the complex problem and finally are used for the further task.

8. Write the advantages and disadvantages of optical fibre.

Ans. The advantages of optical fibre are as follows

(i) These are highly suitable for harsh industrial environment. These are immune to noise caused by electrical and magnetic fields.

(ii) It can support dramatically higher bandwidths (and hence data rates) than either twisted pair or co-axial cable.

(iii) Less signal attenuation.

(iv) These are much lighter than copper cables.

The disadvantages of optical fibre are as follows

(i) These are very difficult to install and maintain.

(ii) They require more protection around the cable than copper cables.

(iii) Propagation of light is uni-directional. For bi-directional communication, two fibres are needed. These are relatively more expensive than other guided media.

9. In a computer lab of a school lab technician is being asked to connect 10 computers, so that students can share their files with each other. What kind of network can be established in school lab?

Ans. Most appropriate network which can be established in Local area network (LAN). LAN is used to cover the small area like a home, office, lab etc.

10. A school wants to start his own education channel on TV to broadcast the computer lectures. Which type of communications will be required to do same?

Ans. Satellite are the most common channel used for telecommunication. They carry TV signals. Therefore, satellite communication will be the most appropriate communication for the school.

11. What are the deployment models of cloud computing?

Ans. The deployment models of cloud computing are as follows

(i) **Private cloud** This type of deployment is used exclusively by a single company or an organization.

(ii) **Public cloud** This is operated by generally third party and any one can be connected with this type of cloud.

(iii) **Hybrid cloud** This type of cloud is a combination of public and private cloud.

12. Compare and contrast the two wireless transmission media–bluetooth and infrared.

Ans. Bluetooth and Infrared both are short range wireless transmission media. This is the only point at which both these data transmission technologies look similar but there is a lot of differences between the two. Infrared is mostly used in TV remotes and there must be a direct line-of-sight between the transmitter and the receiver while on the other hand bluetooth uses a radio frequency which allows transmission through walls and other objects.

13. Explain the following terms.

(i) Bandwidth

(ii) Broadband

Ans. (i) **Bandwidth** It is the communication capacity of a network. It refers to the data carrying capacity of a channel or medium.

(ii) **Broadband** It is a wide bandwidth data transmission with an ability to simultaneously transport multiple signals and traffic types.

14. Differentiate between long distance wireless media and short distance wireless media.

Ans. Differences between long distance wireless media and short distance wireless media are as follows

Long distance wireless media	Short distance wireless media
It supports communication over a long distance, i.e. upto thousands of kilometres.	It supports communication over a short distance, i.e. upto few kilometres.
Microwave, radiowave and satellite communication are long distance wireless media.	Bluetooth, infrared, Wi-Fi, WiMAX are short distance wireless media.

15. Mr Singh and Mr Tyagi want to send a song from each other. Both having a mobile phone. Both want to send a song through mobile phones. What networking technology is needed to share a song through mobile phone? Describe it.

Ans. Bluetooth technology is used for sharing the data like audio, video etc. Using this technology, users of cellular phones, initiate the sending or receiving data.

In general, having all mobiles and fixed computer devices can be totally coordinated. Thus, Mr Singh and Mr Tyagi can send a song to each other by using a bluetooth technology easily within short time.

• Long Answer Type Questions

16. Write in brief, what is the need of computer networking?

Ans. The need of computer networking are as follows

(i) **File and Data Sharing** At a time, file sharing consisted mostly of saving documents to floppy disks that could be physically transferred to other computers by hand. With networking, files can be shared instantaneously across the network, whether with one user or with hundred users. e.g. employees across departments can collaborate on documents, exchange background material etc.

(ii) **Resource Sharing** Computer networking also allows the sharing of network resources, such as printers, scanners, dedicated servers, backup systems, input devices and Internet connections. By sharing resources, unique equipment like scanners, printers etc., can be made available to all network users simultaneously without being relocated, eliminating the need for expensive redundancies.

Data protection and redundancy computer networking allows users to distribute copies of important information across multiple locations, ensuring essential information is not lost with the failure of any one computer in the network. By utilising central backup systems both on-site and off-site, unique documents and data can be gathered automatically from every computer in the network and securely backed up in case of physical computer damage or accidental deletion.

(iii) **Ease of Administration** Instead of individually upgrading each computer in an organisation, a network administrator can initiate an upgrade from a server and automatically duplicate the upgrade throughout the network. Simultaneously, allowing everyone in the company to maintain uniform software, resources and procedures. User communication computer networking also allows organisations to maintain complex communication systems. It also allows users to communicate using E-mail, newsgroups, video conferencing etc.

(iv) **Distributed Computing Power** In computer networks, we can distribute tasks across multiple computers throughout the network, by breaking complex problems into hundreds or thousands of smaller operations, which are then parcelled out to individual computers. Each computer in the network performs its operations on its own portion of the larger problem and return its result. Then, all these results are gathered in such a form that impact as the solution of the complex problem and finally are used for the further task.

(v) **Network Gaming** A lot of network games are available, which allow multi-users to play from different locations. It is a type of online game, i.e. played through social networks.

17. How the Bluetooth is used for network communication? Write the advantages and disadvantages of Bluetooth communication.

Ans. It is a simple, secure and universal wireless communication technology. It refers to a wireless technology that creates small wireless networks, called Personal Area Network (PAN) between PCs and peripheral devices. The bluetooth wireless technology enables you to establish a wireless communication between any two bluetooth devices, such as mobile phones, laptops, cameras or modem stations without any cables. The data transfer rate over the bluetooth varies from 723 Kbps to 1 Mbps in a short range. The standard specification mandates a minimum range of 100 m (328 feet).

The advantages of bluetooth are as follows

(i) It can share data without any wire.

(ii) It consumes low power and low processing.

(iii) It is free to use, if the device is bluetooth enabled.

(iv) Connecting two different devices using bluetooth is very convenient.

The disadvantages of bluetooth are as follows

(i) Only short range communication is possible.

(ii) Connection can be lost under certain conditions.

(iii) It can be easily hacked.

18. What is wireless communication? What kind of communication channels is required for establishing the connection between TV channels?

Ans. Wireless communication channel uses waves to transfer data, i.e. no cables are needed to guide the signals. Hence, this is called unguided media. In this, signals are not bounded to any cabling system, therefore this is also called unbounded media.

These can be categorised as follows

(i) **Long Distance Wireless Media** It supports communication over long distances, i.e. upto thousands of kilometres.

For example, microwave, radiowave, etc.

(ii) **Short Distance Wireless Media** It supports communication over a small distance, generally few miles to a few kilometres.

For example, Infrared, Bluetooth, etc.

For establishing the connection between TV channels we require satellite communication.

Satellites are an essential part of telecommunications systems. They carry a large amount of data in addition to TV signals. When the data is transmitted using satellite, then it is said to be satellite communication. A satellite communication consists of an earth station and a satellite at a stationary orbit, which is about 22300 miles above the earth's surface.

A satellite communication is a space station that receives microwave signals from an earth-based station, amplifies the signals and broadcasts the signals back over a wide area to any number of earth-based stations.

19. What is Wi-Fi communication? Also, write its advantages and disadvantages.

Ans. Wi-Fi stands for Wireless Fidelity, has a range of about 100 m and allows for faster rate between 10-54 Mbps. Wi-Fi services have been introduced for providing high speed Internet access at convenient public locations such as Airports, Universities etc.

Wi-Fi is another name for wireless LAN or WLAN. Home and business networks (private) and public hotspots use it to connect computers and other wireless devices to each other with Internet. Computers and other devices connect to a Wi-Fi network *via* a wireless router or access point.

For Wi-Fi to work, we need

(i) A broadband Internet connection.

(ii) A wireless router.

(iii) A laptop or PC having wireless Internet card or external wireless adapter.

The advantages of Wi-Fi are as follows

(i) It can be used while moving within the signal range.

(ii) Network can be created where you cannot lay cable network. It is a wireless connection that can merge together multiple devices.

The disadvantages of Wi-Fi are as follows

(i) It is more costly than wired network.

(ii) Radiation generated by Wi-Fi can effect human health.

(iii) Power consumption is fairly high.

20. Write the essential characteristics of cloud computing.

Ans. The essential characteristics of cloud computing are as follows

(i) **On Demand self Services** Computer services such as E-mail, applications, network or server service can be accessed without any human interaction.

(ii) **Broad Network Access** Cloud computing provides its services anywhere any time. It is available over internet.

(iii) **Resource Pooling** Cloud is a collection of huge resource pool such as computing power, devices , softwares etc.

(iv) **Rapid Elasticity** Cloud services can be rapidly increased or decreased as per the requirements of the customer.

(v) **Measured Service** All the services provided by cloud computing can be measured, controlled and reported as per the usage only.

21. Carefully read the following descriptions and identify what is being talked about?

(i) It consists of two insulated wires twisted around each other, which provides protection against noise and crosstalk.

(ii) Disturbance caused due to interference of one signal's electric or magnetic field into other signals.

(iii) It is an omni-directional wireless transmission media. Its range lies between 300 KHz to 10 GHz.

(iv) Communication channel that is more secure, faster, easier to set-up but expensive for longer distances and devices once configured cannot be moved.

(v) Unique equipments like printers and scanners are available to all the workstations simultaneously.

Ans. (i) Twisted pair cable

(ii) Crosstalk

(iii) Radiowave

(iv) Wired communication channel

(v) Resource sharing

Chapter Test

Multiple Choice Questions

1. A ....network which can be established for a city or large campus.
    (a) LAN   (b) MAN
    (c) WAN   (d) Internet

2. Full form of PAN is
    (a) Professional Area Net   (b) Personal Area Network
    (c) Peer Area Network   (d) Public Area Net

3. Which wired media is used for long distance?
    (a) Cable   (b) Infrared
    (c) Optical fibre   (d) Phone

4. .... can be used to create a LAN.
    (a) Cable   (b) Bluetooth
    (c) Internet   (d) LAN

5. There are two conductors contain inside .... cables.
    (a) bluetooth   (b) co-axial
    (c) optical Fibre   (d) None of these

6. Which type of cloud can be used by all the users?
    (a) Private cloud   (b) Public cloud
    (c) Hybrid cloud   (d) None of these

Short Answer Type Questions

7. Ramya wants to connect all the computers of her office wirelessly in order to avoid clumsy cables. Which wireless technology would be best suitable for her office? Explain in brief.

8. Explain two problems that can occur during transmission of data.

9. Write down the advantages of networking for an office.

Long Answer Type Questions

10. When we connect computers in a network using cables, then it is called guided media. What are the various types of guided media available? Explain each.

11. Write the applications of cloud computing.

12. What do you mean by a communication channel? What are the types of communication channels?

13. As life gets busy, it becomes difficult for everyone to keep track with school and college friends, old colleagues, old neighbours and favourite teachers. It is important to keep in touch with all your near and dear ones.

At times, people sitting miles away doing similar kind of activity or solving similar kind of problems can help you to achieve goals faster by sharing their experience.

Similarly, people belongs to different socio-economic background can change your perspective and can enhance your understanding of various cultures.

 (i) Suggest any two real-time tools that are suitable for the above mentioned activities.

(ii) What is the generic name used for such tools?

Answers

Multiple Choice Questions

1. (b)   *2. (b)*   *3. (c)*   *4. (a)*   *5. (b)*   *6. (b)*

For Detailed Solutions
Scan the code

CHAPTER 05

Presentation Tools

In this Chapter...

- Starting PowerPoint 2010
- Concept of Slide Show
- Creating New Presentation
- Saving a Presentation
- Different Views of a Slide
- Header and Footer
- Inserting Pictures
- Creating Slide Shows

Presentation is the practice of showing and explaining the content of a topic to an audience or a learner. PowerPoint is a program in MS-Office package with which we can prepare presentations based on slides. PowerPoint helps us in preparing a presentation easily and quickly.

Techniques we use in PowerPoint in preparing slides for making presentations are very similar to techniques used in other programs of MS-Office, such as MS-Word and MS-Excel. Besides this, we can also include information and objects prepared by other programs, such as text, chart worksheet, graphics etc., into the slides of a presentation. PowerPoint saves us a lot of time than to write down the tips on board using chalks or pens. Using PowerPoint, audience will clearly see what's in the presentation, especially when you added some pictures and video clips.

Starting PowerPoint 2010

In order to start working with Microsoft PowerPoint 2010, you will need to locate and open the program on your computer. To open MS-PowerPoint 2010 on your computer, do the following:

Start button → Microsoft Office → Microsoft PowerPoint 2010

MS-PowerPoint 2010 with a blank presentation will be open. By default, the name of a blank presentation is Presentation1.pptx, where .pptx is the extension of MS-PowerPoint 2010 file.

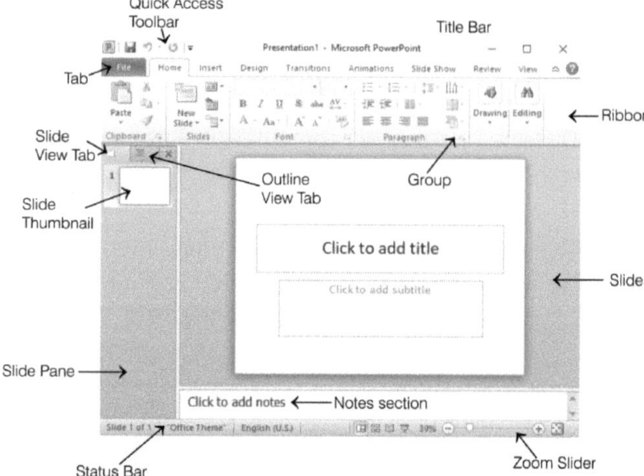

Various components of MS-PowerPoint 2010 window are as follows

(i) **Title bar** It contains the name of currently opened file followed by software name.

(ii) **Ribbon** It is same as Word and Excel, just few tabs are different like Animations, Slide Show etc.

(iii) **Slide** It appears in the centre of the window. You can create your presentation by adding content to the slides.

(iv) **Slide pane** This area of PowerPoint window displays all the slides that are added in the presentation.

(v) **Slides view tab** This tab displays a thumbnail view of all the slides.

(vi) **Outline view tab** This tab displays the text contained in the presentation in an outline format.

(vii) **Notes section** This can be used for creating notes.

(viii) **View buttons** The View buttons appear near the bottom of the screen. It is used to view the changes between Normal view, Slider Sorter view, Reading view and the Slide Show view.

(ix) **Status bar** It displays the number of the slide that is currently being displayed, the total number of slides and the name of the design template which is in use or the name of the background.

Concept of Slide Show

A file created using PowerPoint software is known as Slide. Slide Show refers to the process of running a presentation. In a Slide Show, you can see your presentation in full screen and also run slides in continuous series (one by one). A Slide Show consists of multiple slides. Further, a slide is a combination of graphics, stylised formatting and different types of objects like textboxes, animations, audio and video.

Basic Elements of a Slide

A slide is said to be good, if it conveys the idea in an easy and yet effective manner. In order to create a good slide, understanding of its structure is more important.

Various elements of a slide are as follows

(i) **Title** The heading of a slide is called a title. It represents an idea to the audience about slide contents.

(ii) **Subtitle** The description of the slide data is called a subtitle. It gives more elaborated detail of the central idea of a slide.

(iii) **Text** The entered content by user as bullets on the slide are called text.

(iv) **Drawing objects** The built-in shapes of MS-PowerPoint are called drawing objects.

(v) **ClipArt** The set of built-in pictures provided in MS-PowerPoint gallery are called ClipArt.

(vi) **Media clip** The set of audio, video, animated gif in MS-PowerPoint are called media clip.

(vii) **Pictures** The set of pictures provided in MS-PowerPoint are called pictures.

(viii) **Tables** The collection of rows and columns provided in MS-PowerPoint are called tables.

(ix) **Chart** A graphical representation of data in a slide are called chart.

(x) **SmartArt graphic** The quick way to convert the text in a bulleted list are called SmartArt graphic.

Slide Components used for Reference

Displaying all the information within a slide is not always possible. So, usually a presenter needs additional support like handouts, notes and outlines to display the additional information. These components are used for reference purposes, so that they can help audience to easily get the message conveyed through a presentation. The following components of a slide are used for reference purpose

(i) **Handouts** A smaller version of the slide is called handout. The handout of a presentation, if provided to the audience will help them in understanding the presentation easily.

(ii) **Speaker's notes** The small pictures of slides alongwith some description are called speaker's notes. These are used by the presenter.

(iii) **Outlines** The summarised version of slides in a presentation is called outlines. It consists of only titles and main text of slides and is useful for managing the flow of a presentation.

Slide Layout

It contains formatting, positioning and placeholder boxes for all of the content that appears on a slide. Placeholders are the containers in layout that hold such content as Text (including body text, bulleted lists and titles), Tables, Charts, SmartArt graphics, Movies, Sounds, Pictures and ClipArt and a layout contains the theme (colors, fonts, effects and the background) of a slide as well.

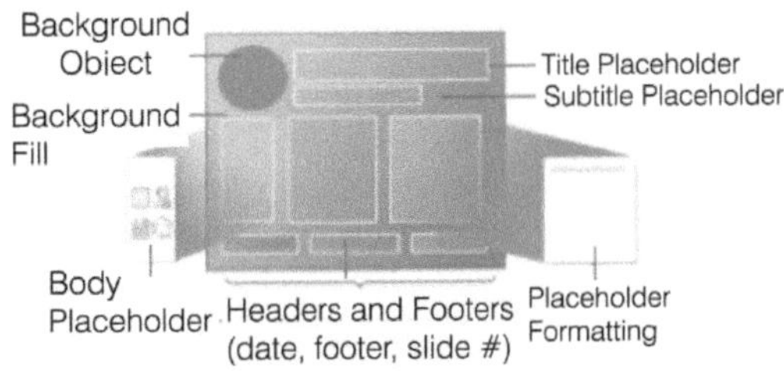

Different Types of Slide Layout

MS-PowerPoint includes nine built-in slide layouts (Standard layouts) or one can create one's custom layouts that meet the specific needs and can share them with other people, who create presentations by using MS-PowerPoint. In given figure, each layout shows the placement of various placeholders in which you will add text or graphics.

(a) **Standard Layouts** The standard, built-in layouts available in Office PowerPoint 2010 are similar to those available in PowerPoint 2003 and earlier versions. When you open a blank presentation in PowerPoint, the default layout called Title Slide (Shown) will appear, but there are other standard layouts that can be applied and used. Other layouts that are present in standard layout are as follows

- Title and Content
- Section Header
- Two Content
- Comparison
- Title Only
- Blank
- Content with Caption
- Picture with Caption

(b) **Custom Layouts** You can create reusable custom layouts that specify the number, size, location of placeholders, background content, theme colors, fonts and effects, optional slide and placeholder level properties.

You can also distribute custom layouts as part of a template, so you no longer have to waste valuable time in cutting and pasting your layouts onto new slides or deleting content on a slide that you want to use with new and different content.

Types of text and object-based placeholders that you can add to build your custom layout include as follows: Content, Text, Pictures, SmartArt graphics, Charts, Tables, Diagrams, Media, Movies and Sound.

Creating New Presentation

For creating a new presentation in MS-PowerPoint, there are two options available to make a selection of creating new presentation.

Creating Blank Presentation

For creating a blank presentation, do the following

(i) Click on File tab and then click New from the menu that appears.

(ii) Select Blank presentation and click on Create button. A blank presentation with one slide will be created. Also, further slides can be added to

the presentation and can change the layout of an existing slide as well.

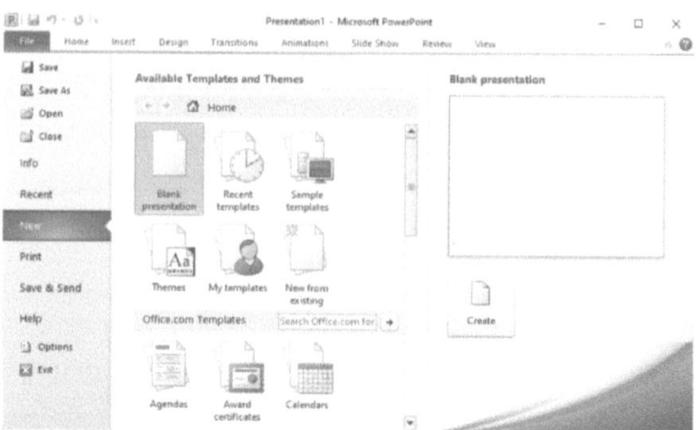

Creating Presentation using Themes

You can quickly and easily format an entire presentation to give it a professional and modern look by applying a theme.

In MS-PowerPoint 2010, you can apply theme using these two methods, which are as follows

Method 1

(i) Click on the File tab and then click on New option.

(ii) Under the Home, select Themes. Available Templates and Themes window will appear.

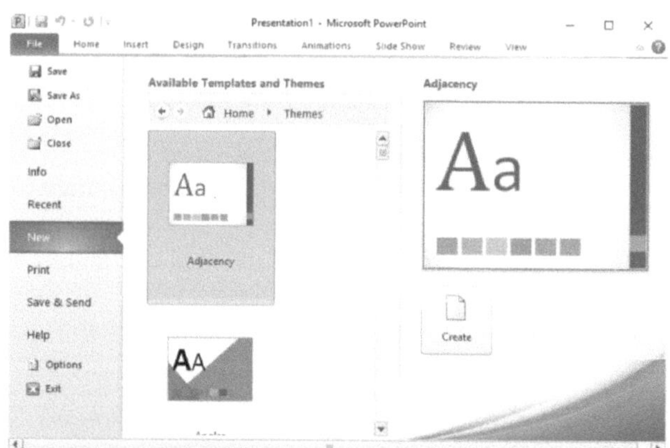

(iii) Select appropriate theme and then click on Create button.

Method 2

(i) Select Design tab under the MS-PowerPoint 2010 ribbon menu system.

(ii) Select any one of the themes as per the user's choice under Themes group.

Saving a Presentation

Procedure for saving a presentation is same as saving a MS-Word document and MS-Excel workbook. For saving your presentation, do the following

(i) Click on the File tab and then click Save As option from the menu that appears.

or Press Ctrl+S keys from keyboard.
(ii) Save As dialog box will appear, in the File name box enter a new name to save the file.
(iii) Then, click Save button.

Different Views of a Slide

In Microsoft Office PowerPoint 2010, different views of a slide are used to edit, print and deliver a presentation. PowerPoint slide views can be found in two places as follows

(i) On the View tab, in the Presentation Views group, where all views are available.
(ii) On an easy-accessible bar, at the bottom of the PowerPoint window, where the main views (Normal, Slide Sorter and Slide Show) are available.

Different types of views available in PowerPoint 2010 are explained below

(a) **Normal View** This is the main editing view, where you write and design your presentations, i.e. actual screen which is displayed. This view is also known as Slide view. A Normal view is the default view size for the screen.

(b) **Slide Sorter View** It provides a view of slides in thumbnail form. This view makes it easy to sort and organise the sequence of the slides at the time of creating presentation and also, at the time of preparing presentation for printing.

(c) **Notes Page View** In this view, the notes pane is located just below the slide pane. Here, notes that apply to the current slide can be typed. Later, these notes can be printed and referred while giving actual presentation. Notes can also be printed to handout to the audience or included in a presentation that is delivered to the audience or posted on a web page.

(d) **Slide Show View** This view is used to deliver a presentation to the audience. Slide Show view takes up the full computer screen, like an actual presentation. In this view, you can see your presentation, the way audience wants. This view enables you to see how graphics, timings, movies, animated effects and transition effects will look during the actual presentation. To exit Slide Show view, press Esc key from the keyboard.

(e) **Master View** This view includes Slide view, Handout view and Notes view. They are the main slides that store information about the presentation, including background color, fonts effects, placeholder sizes and positions. The key benefit to working in a Master view is that on the Slide Master, Notes Master or Handout Master, you can make universal style changes to every slide, notes page or handout associated with the presentation.

Editing and Formatting a Slide

While developing a presentation at some point of time, you may realise the need of changing the content or the outlook of your presentation. MS-PowerPoint 2010 provides you the flexibility of formatting and editing your presentation at any point of time. If you want to make changes in all the slides of your presentation then you should use Slide Sorter View. Otherwise, you can change outlook of individual slides as well.

1. Entering Text

Boxes within a slide layout with dotted borders that contain text and other objects are called placeholders. All built-in slide layouts contain content placeholders, e.g. title text placeholder, subtitle text placeholder, placeholders for pictures, charts, videos etc. To enter text in title and subtitle placeholder, you need to click within these placeholders and enter the text. When you open PowerPoint, title slide will automatically appear. Place cursor in Click to add title text box and insert the derived text in it. Some layout may also have Click to add subtitle.

You can add textbox object in a slide anywhere and then can add text in it. For adding textbox object in your slide, do the following

(i) Select the slide on which you want to insert a textbox.
(ii) Then, click on the Text Box button, under the Insert tab.
(iii) After this, draw a textbox on the slide of whatever length you want.
(iv) Insert the desired text in it.

2. Adding Background

Background styles are variations of background colors derived from combinations of themes, colors and background intensities in the current document theme. For changing the background of presentation, you have to choose a different background style. For applying or changing the background of a presentation, do the following

(i) Click the slide or slides on which you want to add a background style.
(ii) To select multiple slides, click the first slide and then press and hold Ctrl key while you click the other slides.
(iii) On the Design tab, in the Background group, click the arrow next to the Background Styles.
(iv) Right-click on the background style that you want to apply and then do one of the following
(a) To apply the background style to the selected slides, click Apply to Selected Slides.
(b) To apply the background style to all of the slides in your presentation, click Apply to All Slides.

3. Adding Watermark

You can insert a picture, including ClipArt behind part of your slide as a watermark. By adding a picture as a watermark to one or all of your slides, can make your Microsoft Office PowerPoint 2010 presentation unique or clearly identify your presentation sponsor. You can lighten your picture, ClipArt or color so that, it does not interfere with the content of your slide. You can also use Text or WordArt as a watermark to indicate that your presentation is a draft or confidential.

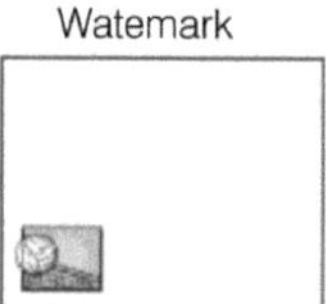

Watermarks are flexible because you can change their sizes and their position on a slide. You can apply a watermark to some or all of the slides in your presentation.

Use Picture or ClipArt as a Watermark

To use a picture or ClipArt as a watermark, do the following

  (i) Click the slide on which you want to add a watermark. On the View tab, in the Master Views group, click Slide Master.

  (ii) On the Insert tab, in the Images group, do one of the following:

To use a picture as a watermark, click Picture option, locate the picture that you want to apply and then click Insert button.

or

To use ClipArt as a watermark, click ClipArt. In the ClipArt task pane, in the Search for box, either type a word or phrase that describes the clip that you want, or type all or part of the file name of the clip and then click Go button. Now, insert any ClipArt which you want.

  (iii) To adjust the size of the picture or ClipArt, right-click the picture or ClipArt on the slide and then click Size and Position… option from the drop down menu. A Format Picture dialog box will appear.

  (iv) On the Size tab, under Scale, increase or decrease the settings in the Height and Width boxes.

  (v) To move the picture or ClipArt on the slide, click the Position tab and then enter the settings for the positions that you want in the Horizontal and Vertical boxes and then click on Close button.

  (vi) Under Picture Tools Format tab, in the Adjust group, click color and then under more.

Variations, click the color fade that you want.

  (vii) Under Picture Tools Format tab, in the Adjust group, click corrections and then click the brightness percentage that you want.

  (viii) When you finish editing and positioning the watermark and are satisfied with its appearance, to send the watermark to the back of the slide, under Picture Tools Format tab, in the Arrange group, click Send to Back from send Backward.

Use Textbox or WordArt as Watermark

To use a textbox or WordArt as a watermark, do the following

  (i) Click the slide that you want to add a textbox or WordArt as watermark.

  (ii) On the Insert tab, in the Text group, do one of the following:

To use a textbox, click Text Box.

or To use a WordArt, click WordArt.

  (iii) Enter text in the textbox or WordArt that you want to appear in the watermark.

  (iv) If you want to reposition the watermark, click the textbox or WordArt and then when the pointer becomes a ✛ , drag the textbox or WordArt to a new location.

  (v) When you finish editing and positioning the watermark and are satisfied with its appearance, to send the textbox or WordArt to the back of the slide, under Drawing Tools Format tab, in the Arrange group, click Send to Back from send Backward.

Header and Footer

When it is required to add text (such as your presentation's title, the presenter's name, a file name, company name and many more) to the bottom of one or more slides, handouts or notes pages in a presentation or to the top of one or more handouts or notes pages in a presentation, concept of header and footer is used.

Add a Footer to a Slide

To add a footer to a slide, do the following

  (i) On the Insert tab, in the Text group, click Header & Footer option.

  (ii) A Header and Footer dialog box will appear.

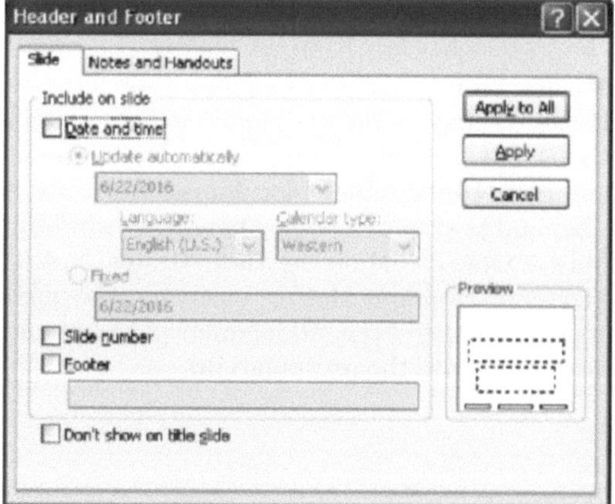

(iii) In the Header and Footer dialog box, on the Slide tab, select the Footer check box and then type the text that you want to appear in the centre bottom of the slide.

(iv) To keep the text in the footer from appearing on the title slide, select the Don't show on title slide check box.

(v) Do one of the following

To display footer information on the selected slide only, click Apply.

or To display footer information on all the slides in your presentation, click Apply to All.

Add a Header, Footer or both to a Handouts or Notes Page

For adding a header and footer to a handouts or notes page, do the following

(i) On the Insert tab, in the Text group, click Header & Footer option.

A Header and Footer dialog box will appear.

(ii) In the Header and Footer dialog box, on the Notes and Handouts tab, select the Header or Footer check box or both and then type the text that you want to appear in the centre top (header) or centre bottom (footer) of each notes page or handouts.

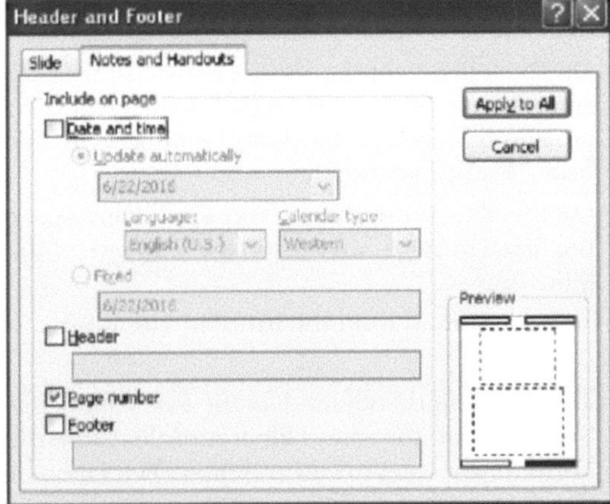

(iii) Click Apply to All.

Note *The Preview box, located in the Header and Footer dialog box, displays the Header and Footer information in the location that the slide, handout or notes page will display it.*

Adding Slide Numbers and Date/Time to a Slide

Slide numbers, notes page numbers, handouts page numbers, the date and time can all be added to a presentation.

1. Add Slide Page Numbers

For adding page numbers to the slides of your presentation, do the following

(i) On the View tab, in the Presentation Views group, click Normal and then on the slide pane that contains

the Slides and Outline tabs, click the first slide thumbnail in your presentation.

(ii) Now, click on the Insert tab, in the Text group, click Slide Number option.

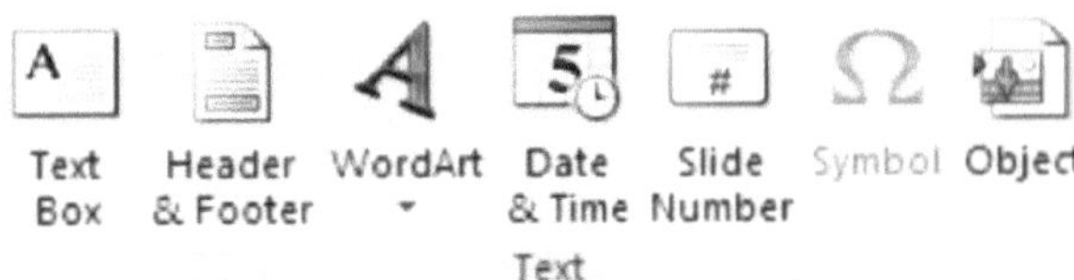

(iii) A Header and Footer dialog box will appear.

(iv) In the Header and Footer dialog box, do one of the following:

If you want to add slide numbers, click the Slide tab and then select the Slide number check box.

or

If you want to add page numbers to notes or handouts, click the Notes and Handouts tab and then select the Page number check box.

(v) Click Apply to All.

2. Timing Text Box or Add Date and Time

For adding date and time to the slide, do the following

(i) On the View tab, in the Presentation Views group, click Normal and then on the slide pane that contains the Slides and Outline tabs, click the first slide thumbnail in your presentation.

(ii) On the Insert tab, in the Text group, click Date & Time option. A Header and Footer dialog box will appear.

(iii) In the Header and Footer dialog box, do one of the following:

If you want to add the date and time to your slides, click the Slide tab.

or

If you want to add the date and time to your notes pages or handouts, click the Notes and Handouts tab.

(iv) Select the Date and time check box and then, do one of the following:

By default the Update automatically radio button selected that reflect the current date and time, each time when you open or print the presentation, click Update automatically and then select the date and time format that you want.

or

If you want to set the date and time to a specific date, click Fixed radio button and then in the text box, type the date that you want.

Note *By setting the date on your presentation, so that it is fixed, you can easily keep track of the last time you made changes to it.*

(v) If you want to add the date and time to all of the slides, notes pages or handouts in your presentation, click Apply to All.

Inserting Pictures

Pictures and ClipArt can be inserted into a Microsoft PowerPoint 2010 presentation from sources such as ClipArt Website providers, web pages or files on a computer. These pictures can be used as backgrounds for slides in a presentation.

For inserting pictures from file in your presentation, do the following

  (i) Click where you want to insert the picture.

  (ii) On the Insert tab, in the Images group, click Picture option.

  (iii) Locate the picture that you want to insert and then double click on it.

or

To add multiple pictures, press and hold Ctrl key while you click the pictures that you want to insert and then click Insert button.

Note *To insert a picture into the notes pages of an Office PowerPoint 2010 presentation, switch to Notes view and then do the above same procedure.*

Creating Slide Shows

Using PowerPoint, a wide range of special effects, such as transition and animation can be added in a presentation to provide visual interest to the presentation and grab the audience's attention. Points can be revealed on slides in a staggered way (i.e. one bullet displayed at a time) to keep the audience focused only on the point which is being discussed at the given time. Also, the presentation can be automated, so it runs on its own.

The slide show can be enhanced by applying the following effects

Adding Transitions to a Slide

Slide transitions are the animation-like effects that occur in Slide Show view while moving from one slide to the next during an on-screen presentation. The speed of each slide transition effect can be controlled and sound effects can also be added to a slide. PowerPoint supports with different types of built-in transition effects like cut, dissolve, wipe down and many more.

Adding different slide transitions to the slides in your presentation, do the following

  (i) On the left side of the slide window, in the pane that contains the Slides and Outline tabs, click the Slides tab and then select a slide thumbnail.

  (ii) On the Transitions tab, in the Transition to This Slide group, select any Slide Transition Effect that you want for that slide.

  (iii) To set the slide transition speed between the current slide and the next slide, in the Timing group, click the arrow next to Duration and then select the speed that you want.

  (iv) To add a different slide transition to another slide in your presentation, repeat steps (i) to (iii).

Adding the same slide transition to all of the slides in your presentation, do the following

  (i) On the left side of the slide window, in the pane that contains the Slides and Outline tabs, click the Slides tab.

  (ii) Select the slide thumbnail of the slides that you want to apply slide transitions.

  (iii) On the Transitions tab, in the Transition to This Slide group, select any Effect options.

  (iv) To set the slide transition speed between the current slide and the next slide, in the Timing group, click the arrow next to Duration and then select the speed that you want.

  (v) In the Timing group, click Apply to All.

Add Sound to Slide Transitions

For adding sound to the slide transitions, do the following

  (i) On the left side of the slide window, in the pane that contains the Slides and Outline tabs, click the Slides tab and then select the slide thumbnails that you want to add a sound to.

  (ii) On the Transitions tab, in the Timing group, click the arrow next to Sound and then do one of the following:

To add a sound from the list, that you want.

or

To add a sound not found on the list, select Other Sound, locate the sound file from Add Audio dialog box that you want to add and then click Open button.

  (iii) To add sound to a different slide transitions, repeat step (ii).

Animating Text and Objects

We can give sound effects or visual effects, including movement to the text or objects in a presentation. Animation can be used to focus on important points, to control the flow of information and to increase viewer interest in a presentation. Built-in animation effect can be added in PowerPoint 2010 presentation by doing the following

  (i) Select the text or object that you want to animate.

  (ii) On the Animations tab, in the Animation group, select the animation effect that you want from the Animate list.

Rehearse Timing

This option is used to control the speed of the transition and animation effects that have been applied to the slide. Using this feature, the amount of time you spend on each slide is recorded while rehearsing for the presentation and that timing can be used to run the Slide Show automatically in future.

For using this outstanding feature, do the following

(i) On the Slide Show tab, in the Set Up group, click Rehearse Timings.

The Rehearsal toolbar will appear and the Recording box begins timing the presentation.

(ii) While you set the time in your presentation, do one or more of the following on the Rehearsal toolbar

(a) To move the next slide, click Next.

(b) To temporarily stop recording the time, click Pause Recording.

(c) To restart recording the time after pausing, click Resume Recording.

(d) To restart recording the time for the current slide, click Repeat.

(iii) After you set the time for the last slide, a message box displays the total time for the presentation and prompts you to do one of the following:

To keep the recorded slide timings, click Yes.

or

To discard the recorded slide timings, click No. Slide Sorter View will appear and display the time of each slide in your presentation.

Chapter Practice

Objective Questions

• Multiple Choice Questions

1. .... is the default file name for a PowerPoint presentation.
   (a) Untitled1   (b) Book1
   (c) Presentation1   (d) Document1

Ans. (*c*) The default name given to a presentation file is Presentation1.

2. File extension for a PowerPoint 2010 presentation is
   (a) .ptt   (b) .pptx
   (c) .docx   (d) .clsx

Ans. (*b*) .pptx is the file extension given to all PowerPoint 2010 files.

3. The custom animation can apply
   (a) Font work gallery (b) Gallery
   (c) Text   (d) All of these

Ans. (*d*) The custom animation can be applied on font work gallery, gallery and text.

4. Professional looking visual aids are prepared with the help of software called ..... .
   (a) DBMS
   (b) multimedia
   (c) graphics software
   (d) presentation graphics software

Ans. (*d*) Professional looking visual aids are prepared with the help of software called presentation graphics software.

5. A set of predefined formats of text or color scheme is called
   (a) slide   (b) presentation scheme
   (c) theme   (d) schema

Ans. (*c*) A set of predefined formats of text or color scheme is called theme.

6. Which of the following views is useful for representing the structure of a presentation?
   (a) Notes view   (b) Outline view
   (c) Slide view   (d) Normal view

Ans. (*b*) Outline view is useful for checking the flow or structure of a presentation.

7. The entire presentation can be seen at a time in
   (a) Slide Show view
   (b) Outline view
   (c) Normal view
   (d) Slide Sorter view

Ans. (*d*) Slide Sorter view enables you to view the entire presentation at a time.

8. Which among the following views allows you to give a thumbnail view of all the slides in a presentation?
   (a) Normal view   (b) Outline view
   (c) Notes view   (d) Slide Sorter view

Ans. (*d*) Slide Sorter view provides a view of slides in thumbnail form.

9. Which among the following views allows you to add some extra information to a slide which is not viewed during the presentation?
   (a) Normal view   (b) Outline view
   (c) Notes Page view   (d) Slide Sorter view

Ans. (*c*) Notes Page view allows you to add some extra information related to presentation but it is not viewed during the presentation.

10. Which file format can be added to a PowerPoint show?
   (a) .jpg   (b) .gif
   (c) .wav   (d) All of these

Ans. (*d*) .jpg and .gif are file extensions for images and .wav is an extension for video file. Hence, all given formats are supported in PowerPoint.

11. Rama is preparing a presentation on her company's annual performance. She wants some text present on a slide to fly in from the left, when she clicks the mouse. Which of the following features should she use?
   (a) Slide Show
   (b) Slide Transition
   (c) Custom Animation
   (d) Text Animation

Ans. (*c*) Custom Animation can be used for the desired functionality.

12. Special effects used to introduce slides in a presentation are

(a) transitions   (b) effects

(c) custom animations   (d) annotations

Ans. (*a*) Special effects used to introduce slides in a presentation are known as transitions.

13. Rehearse Timings command is present on .... tab.

(a) Animations   (b) Review

(c) Slide Show   (d) View

Ans. (*c*) Rehearse Timings command is present on Slide Show tab.

14. To set new timing while rehearsing, ... key is pressed.

(a) Ctrl+T   (b) T   (c) M   (d) O

Ans. (*b*) T key is used to set new timing while rehearsing.

15. What is the shortcut key to display the Microsoft PowerPoint shortcut menu?

(a) F7   (b) F8   (c) Shift+F10   (d) F11

Ans. (*c*) Shift + F10 is the shortcut key to display the PowerPoint shortcut menu.

• Case Based MCQs

Direction *Read the case and answer the following questions.*

16. PowerPoint is similar to a word processor, except that it's geared toward creating presentations rather than documents. PowerPoint presentations consist of one or more slides. Each slide can contain text, graphics and other information. You can easily rearrange the slides in a PowerPoint presentation, delete slides that you don't need, add new slides, or modify the contents of existing slides. A PowerPoint presentation can share important information such as a business plan or educational lesson, or it can be useful for entertainment purposes. You have a lot of control over customising a PowerPoint presentation and can start quickly with templates and a variety of useful tools.

(i) Presentation is the process of .... a required topic to audience.

(a) displaying   (b) printing

(c) presenting   (d) listening

(ii) A theme of presentation is defined as predefined combination of colors, effects and

(a) video   (b) images   (c) size   (d) fonts

(iii) The traditional way of presenting information to people was to stand at the front of a room armed with set of ....

(a) slides   (b) screen

(c) camera   (d) notes

(iv) To software that is used to make presentation easy and visualise is called

(a) MS-Word   (b) MS-PowerPoint

(c) MS-Excel   (d) WordPad

(v) Using presentation software which cannot be added to the presentations?

(a) SmartArt   (b) Images

(c) Animations   (d) None of these

Ans. (i) (*c*) The presentation is a process of presenting any topic to the required audience.

(ii) (*d*) A presentation theme in presentation software is a predefined combination of colors, fonts and effects that can be applied to presentation.

(iii) (*d*) A traditional way of presenting information was stand in front of the room and armed with set of notes.

(iv) (*b*) The MS-PowerPoint is software which is used to make presentation easy and more visualise.

(v) (*d*) Using presentation we can add almost everything such as : SmartArt, Animations, Images, Videos etc.

PART 2
Subjective Questions

• Short Answer Type Questions

1. How many views of a slide PowerPoint are provided? Name them.

Ans. There are six views in PowerPoint. They are as follows

(i) Normal view   (ii) Outline view

(iii) Notes Page view   (iv) Slide Show view

(v) Slide Sorter view   (vi) Master view

2. State three functions of the Slides Pane.

Ans. Three functions of the Slides Pane are as follows

(i) New slides may be added to the presentation.

(ii) Allows marking a slide as hidden for not showing it during a Slide Show.

(iii) Deleting a slide from the presentation in case it is no longer needed.

3. Write three functions that can be performed in Slide Sorter view of a presentation.

Ans. The three functions that can be performed in Slide Sorter view are as follows

(i) We can see the entire presentation.

(ii) We can move slide from one place to another using click-drag method. Also, we can rearrange the order of slides.

(iii) We can insert, rename and delete slides.

4. How are Header and Footer useful?

Ans. Header and Footer are very useful for displaying the similar useful information (such as presenter's name, file name, company name, presentation's title and many more) on each slide. One can change the Header and Footer details at any time in the presentation.

5. What is a Slide Sorter view?

Ans. The Slide Sorter view is useful for the viewing of the slides in miniature form and can be helpful is evaluating all the slides at the same time and also in rearranging them.

6. What is presentation software?

Ans. Presentation software is a specialised type of graphics software, which is used to create professional looking visual aids for an audience. The visual aids can be computer images, photographic transparencies, etc. Using this software one can create Slide Show, which are in electronic form of the presentation and can be shown using projector or on computer screen.

7. Write the name of some of the basic elements of the slide.

Ans. Some of the basic elements of the slide are as follows

  (i) Title and Sub-title

  (ii) Charts and Graphs

  (iii) Drawing objects and Shapes

  (iv) ClipArt and SmartArt

  (v) Audio and Video

8. What do you understand by a presentation theme?

Ans. A presentation theme is a predefined set of colors, fonts, etc. These effects can be easily applied to a presentation and give the consistent and professional look.

9. Differentiate Normal view and Slide Sorter view of the presentations.

Ans. **Normal view** is the main editing view, where you write and design your presentations. Normal view has four working areas. In **Slide Sorter view** gives you a view of your slides in thumbnail form. This view makes it easy for you to sort and organise the sequence of your slides as you create your presentation, and then also as you prepare your presentation for printing.

10. What is the difference between Slide and Slide Show?

Ans. **Slide** A Slide is a single page of a presentation. Collectively, a group of slides may be known as a slide deck.

  Slide Show A Slide Show is an exhibition of a series of slides or images in an electronic device or in a projection screen.

11. Write steps to navigate between slides in Normal View.

Ans. To navigate between slides in Normal View, steps are

Step 1 Click the Normal View button.

Step 2 Click a Slide in the left pane and drag and drop it to its new location.

Step 3 Hold down the left mouse button and drag the Slide to its new location. A pointer with a box appears as you drag the Slide.

Step 4 Release the mouse button where you want to place the slide.

12. Write steps to change Slide Sorter view to Normal view.

Ans. You can switch to Slide Sorter view in two easy ways:

Step 1 Click the Slide Sorter button at the right side of the status bar.

Step 2 Select the View tab on the Ribbon and then click the Slide Sorter button in the Presentation Views group.

13. Write the steps of inserting picture in a Slide.

Ans. Following are three steps of inserting picture in a Slide

Step 1 Click at the place where you want to insert a picture.

Step 2 Click on the Insert tab, in the Images group and then click on Picture option.

Step 3 Select the picture that you want to insert and double click on it.

or

If you wish to add multiple pictures then press and hold Ctrl key, while you click the pictures that you want to insert and then click Insert button.

14. Differentiate between Slide Transition and Custom Animation.

Ans. (i) Slide Transitions are the looks that take you from one slide to the next, while Custom Animations are the movements you put on text, pictures, objects on an individual slide.

  (iii) Slide Transitions are applied to slides themselves, while Custom Animations are applied to objects on a slide.

• Long Answer Type Questions

15. Ketan is preparing a presentation for his new product promotion.

  (i) The content is ready but he has no time to design backgrounds and decide on color scheme for the presentation. Name the features that will help him to create a professional presentation without devoting much time.

  (ii) He wants to set how a slide appears and disappears on screen when he runs the slide show. Which feature should he use?

Ans. (i) He has to take the help of master pages from taskpane to set a suitable background which supports descent color background.

  (ii) He must have to set some slide transition and custom animation effect from taskpane.

16. A sales manager creates a presentation, he adds the same slide transition to all the slide. Write steps, which are followed by sales manager for slide transition.

Ans. He used an option called as Rehearse Timing. This option is used to control the speed of the transition of the slides. Following steps can be used to add transitions-

Step 1 Click on the Slide Show tab, in the Set Up group, select Rehearse Timings option. The Rehearsal toolbar will appear and the Recording box begins timing the presentation.

Step 2 For setting the time in your presentation, do one or more of the following on the Rehearsal toolbar

(a) To move the next slide, click Next.

(b) For temporarily stop recording the time, click Pause Recording.

(c) To restart recording the time after pausing, click Resume Recording.

(d) To restart recording the time for the current slide, click Repeat.

Step 3 After completion of the time setting of the last slide, a message box displays the total time for the presentation and prompts you to do one of the following

To keep the recorded slide timings, click Yes.

or

To discard the recorded slide timings, click No. Slide Sorter View will appear and display the time of each slide in your presentation.

17. What are the different ways in which you can create a new presentation? Write steps for each.

Ans. There are two ways of creating new presentation

Blank Presentation without Themes

The new Blank Presentation can be created by using following steps

Step 1 First click on File tab and then select New from the menu that appears.

Step 2 Select Blank presentation and click on Create button.

A blank presentation with one slide will be created. Also, further new slides can be added to the presentation and can change the layout of an existing slide as well.

Blank Presentation with Themes

We can quickly and easily format an entire presentation to give it a professional and modern look by using a theme. In PowerPoint, there are two methods for applying theme.

Method 1

(i) Click on File tab and then select New from the menu that appears.

(ii) Under the Home, select Themes. Available Templates and Themes window will appear.

(iii) Select appropriate theme and then click on create button.

Method 2

(i) Select Design tab from Ribbon menu system.

(ii) Select any one of the themes as per the user's choice under Themes group.

Effects will be automatically applied on all the slides.

18. Explain Notes Page view, Slide Show view and Master view of presentation.

Ans. **Notes Page View** In this view, the notes pane is located just below the slide pane. Here, notes that apply to the current slide can be typed. Further, these notes can be printed and referred while giving actual presentation. Notes can also be printed to handout to the audience or included in a presentation that is delivered to the audience or posted on a web page.

Slide Show View This view is used to deliver a presentation to the audience. Slide show view takes up the full computer screen, like an actual presentation. In this view, you can see your presentation, the way audience wants. This view enables you to see how graphics, timings, movies, animated effects and transition effects will look during the actual presentation. To exit Slide Show View, press Esc key from the keyboard.

Master View This view includes Slide View, Handout View and Notes View. They are the main slides that store information about the presentation, including background color, fonts effects, placeholder sizes and positions. The key benefit to working in a Master View is that on the Slide Master, Notes Master or Handout Master, you can make universal style changes to every slide, notes page or handout associated with the presentation.

19. Write the steps to add background in the presentation.

Ans. We can add different type of background styles in the presentation. Background styles are variations of background colors derived from combinations of themes, colors and background intensities in the current document theme. For changing the background of presentation, you have to choose a different background style. For applying or changing the background of a presentation, following steps can be used

Step 1 Click the slide or slides on which you want to add a background style.

Step 2 To select multiple slides, click the first slide and then press and hold Ctrl key while you click the other slides.

Step 3 On the Design tab, in the Background group, click the arrow next to the Background Styles.

Step 4 Right click on the background styles that you want to apply and then do one of the following

(a) To apply the background style to the selected slides, click Apply to Selected Slides.

(b) To apply the background style to all of the slides in your presentation, click Apply to All Slides.

Chapter Test

Multiple Choice Questions

1. Which of the following statement is not true?
(a) You can directly type the text in the blank slide.
(b) From Insert menu choose Picture and then Image file to insert your image in the slide.
(c) You can view PowerPoint presentation in Normal View, Slide Show View and Slide Sorter View.
(d) All of the above

2. Which of the following section is not available in slide layout?
(a) Titles   (b) Lists   (c) Charts   (d) Animations

3. An electronic page in the presentation is called
(a) page   (b) E-page   (c) slide   (d) notes

4. Which of the following is not a view of PowerPoint?
(a) Slide Sorter view   (b) Slide view   (c) Sort view   (d) Slide Show view

5. A predefined formats of text or color scheme is called as
(a) slide   (b) templates   (c) presentation scheme   (d) slide show

6. From .... page, it is possible for you to choose slide designs.
(a) Slide Sorter view   (b) Slide view   (c) Slide Show view   (d) All of these

7. What is Slide Transition?
(a) A special effect used to introduce a slide during a Slide Show.
(b) A special effect that controls the degree to which the colors on one side of a slide can change to some other color on the other slide.
(c) A common feature that allows a slide to be easily copied into another PowerPoint presentations.
(d) All of the above

Short Answer Type Questions

8. What can you do, if you want each slide should be shown for a specific amount of time?

9. Mala is working as marketing manager in an advertising company. She has prepared a presentation on her latest product. What feature will be used for the following tasks?
(i) To view all slides together.
(ii) To set timings of the slide show while rehearsing.
(iii) To show the sales using a chart.

10. What is the use of header and footer in the presentation?

11. Seema wants to give identical design to all the slides and handouts, she is going to print from her presentation. Which two methods can she use to accomplish her task?

Long Answer Type Questions

12. What are various slide components which can be used for reference?

13. What are the basic elements of a slide?

14. Suman is working as marketing manager in an advertising company. She has prepared a presentation on her latest product. What feature will be used for the following tasks?
(i) Represent the data in graphical form.
(ii) Notes provided to audience to understand the presentation.
(iii) Shows the slides up the full computer screen.
(iv) Control the speed of the transition.
(v) Represent the data in tabular form.

Answers

Multiple Choice Questions

1. (a)   2. (d)   3. (c)   4. (c)   5. (b)   6. (b)   7. (a)

For Detailed Solutions
Scan the code

CHAPTER 06

Spreadsheet Tools

In this Chapter...

- Opening of MS-Excel
- Working with a Spreadsheet
- Auto Fill : A Range
- Changing Font, Size and Color
- Formatting Text
- Formatting Numbers
- Inserting/Deleting Cells, Rows and Columns
- Working with Formulas and Functions
- Working with Charts
- Printing a Worksheet/Workbook

A spreadsheet is a configuration of rows and columns. Rows are horizontal vectors while columns are vertical vectors. A spreadsheet is also known as a worksheet. Spreadsheet program also provides tools for creating graphs and inserting pictures etc., for analysing the data.

Microsoft Excel is a spreadsheet application program offered in the Microsoft Office software package that runs on a personal computer. It is very useful for storing, organising, manipulating and retrieving data.

Opening of MS- Excel

In order to start working with Microsoft Excel, you need to locate and open the program on your computer. To open MS-Excel on your computer, do the following

Click on Start button → Microsoft Office → Microsoft Excel 2010

It will open MS-Excel with a blank spreadsheet. By default, the name of a blank spreadsheet is Book1.xlsx, where .xlsx is the extension of MS-Excel. Figure shows the blank spreadsheet and its major parts.

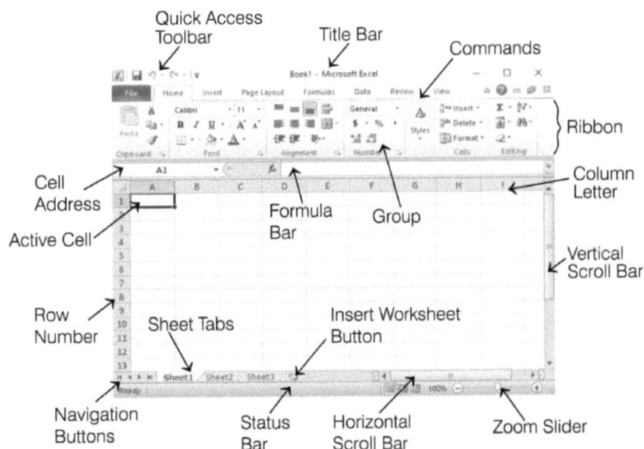

The major components of MS-Excel window are as follows

(i) **File tab** This tab is found at the top-left corner of the window. When you left-click on the tab, a menu will appear. From this menu, you can create a new spreadsheet, open existing files, save files in a variety of ways and print.

(ii) **Quick access toolbar** On the top-left hand side of the Title bar, you will see several little icons above the ribbon menu system. These let you perform common tasks, such as saving and undoing, without opening menus.

(iii) **Title bar** The bar located at the top of the active window is called Title bar. It contains the name of the currently open document.

(iv) **Ribbon menu system** The ribbon is the panel at the top portion of the document. It has 8 tabs and each tab is divided into various groups. These groups are logical collections of features designed to perform various functions that you will utilise in developing or editing your Excel sheets.

(v) **Equation editor** It is generally found below the ribbon menu. The left side denotes which cell is selected ('A1'), where 'A' represents first row and '1' represents first column. It is also called as Cell Address and the right side allows you to input equations or text into the selected cell, called Formula Bar.

(vi) **Worksheet** The primary document that you use in Microsoft Excel to store and work with data is a worksheet or sheet. A worksheet is always stored in a workbook. The number of sheets can be increased or decreased as per requirement using Insert Worksheet option or shift + F11.

Excel Workbook

When we open Excel then the file opened is called as a workbook. A workbook consists of many worksheets. It is suggested to create a single workbook with various worksheets to keep a particular task together.

For example, A teacher wish to save marks of different section for a subject Math. He/She can create a workbook with number of worksheets with respect to each section and save marks of Math subject.

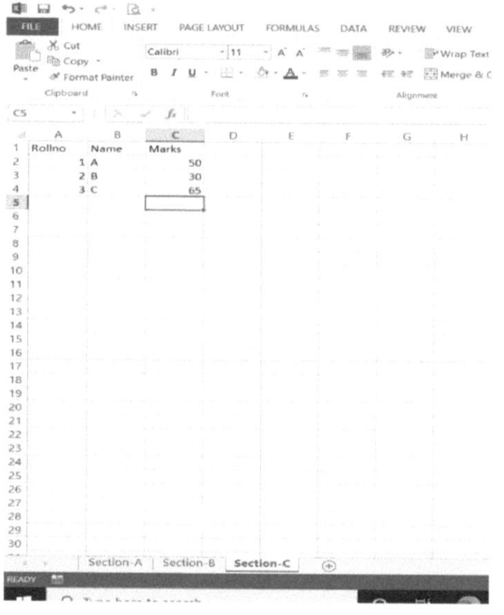

- **New workbook** New workbook can be created by selecting File tab →New workbook→ Blank workbook.
- **Open existing workbook** Existing workbook can be opened by selecting File tab → Open.
- **Save workbook** Current workbook can be saved by selecting File tab → Save or Save As or same can be done by quick panel also.

Excel Worksheet

By default in a workbook, there are three sheets available namely Sheet1, Sheet2 and Sheet to users. You can add further sheets in a workbook. The maximum number of sheets allowed in a workbook is limited by the amount of memory available on your computer.

- To add a new worksheet, click the Insert Worksheet tab at the bottom of the screen.
- To rename a worksheet- double click on the sheet name (Sheet1) and rename it.
- Deleting One or More Worksheets- You can also delete more than one worksheet from a workbook by doing the following
  (i) Select the worksheet or worksheets that you want to delete. (For selecting multiple sheets at a time, press and hold Shift key).
  (ii) You can right click on sheet and choose Delete command from menu.

Working with a Spreadsheet

MS-Excel allows you to entering data, copy and paste cells and cell content through cutting and pasting or copying and pasting.

Entering Data in a Cell

MS-Excel is extremely powerful for entering, storing, displaying and manipulating different kinds of data efficiently. There are three main types of data, i.e. text, numbers and date/time that can be entered and stored in the cells.

- To enter a text in a cell, do the following
  (i) Select the cell in which you want to enter text.
  (ii) Start typing the text.
  (iii) Press the Enter key.
- To enter a number in a cell, do the following
  (i) Select a cell, where you want to type a number.
  (ii) Type the number. You can use %, (,), ., $ etc., in the number.
  (iii) Press the Enter key.
- To enter date/time in a cell, do the following
  (i) Select the cell, where you want to type a date/time.
  (ii) Type date/time.
  (iii) When you type a date/time, Excel converts your data to a serial number. The serial number

represents the number of days from the beginning of the century until the date you type.

(iv) To format those cells in date/time format, click Short Date or Long Date or Time Format, respectively from the number format list.

(v) After a cell has been formatted in date or time format, date/time will be in general form, i.e. dd/mm/yy, HH: MM : SS format.

Cut, Copy and Paste Options

Copy range of Cells- A range of cells may contain a single cell or a group of cells. Basically, it is a group of contiguous cells forming a rectangular area of cells. When we select a cell, its name gets displayed in the Name Box of the Equation Editor.

Similarly, the name of the selected range of cells also gets displayed in the same Name Box. e.g. a range starting from E3 till G15 would be written as E3:G15. Here, colon (:) represents the range indicator. We can do this in two ways, through keyboard and mouse. Shortcut keys for Copy, Cut and Paste are – Ctrl+C , Ctrl+X and Ctrl+V, respectively.

Auto Fill : A Range

MS-Excel supports with an excellent and time saving feature called AutoFill. Using this feature, you do not need to fill manually pattern specific data series in multiple cells in a sequence. There are two methods of using this feature

- **Method 1 Using Fill Handle.**

  Type the two values in a column or row and by using fill handing drag the cursor till end of the series with the help of a mouse.

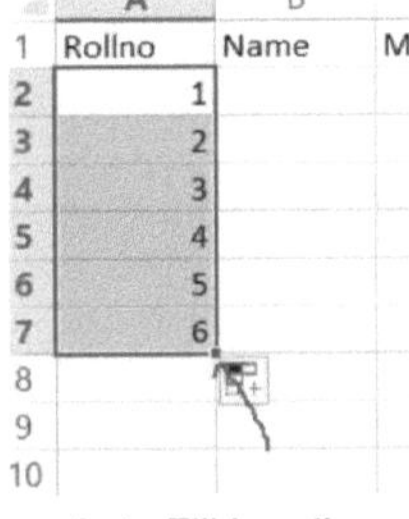

Auto Fill handle

- **Method 2** Auto fill of series can be done using fill button available in editing group.

Auto fill by fill option in editing group

Changing Font, Size and Color

In Excel, you can change the font, size and color of the cell content in the same way as you have done in MS-Word 2010. For changing the font color of the cell content, do the following

(i) Select the cell or range of cells that you want to format.

(ii) Locate the Font group under the Home tab.

(iii) Click on the down-facing arrow next to the Font Color menu.

(iv) From the list that appears, select the color that you want.

For changing the font size of the cell content, do the following

(i) Select the cell or range of cells that you want to format.

(ii) Locate the Font group under the Home tab.

(iii) Click on the down-facing arrow next to the Font Size menu.

(iv) From the list that appears, click on any size of the font that you want.

For changing the font type of the cell content, do the following

(i) Select the cell or range of cells that you want to format.

(ii) Locate the Font group under the Home tab.

(iii) Click on the down-facing arrow next to the Font menu.

(iv) From the list that appears, click on any type of the font that you want.

Formatting Text

Formatting of text involves so many things, i.e. we can format text in terms of alignment, orientation, wrapping and merging.

Cell Alignment

By default, all cell contents are aligned to the bottom of the cell, texts are aligned to the left of a cell and numbers are aligned to the right of a cell.

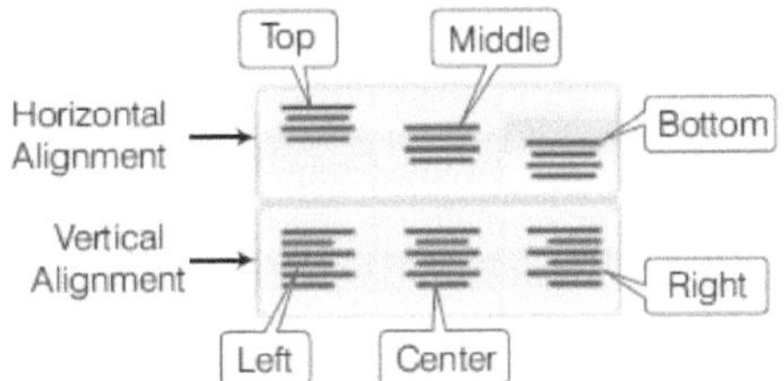

To change the alignment of the contents of a cell, do the following

(i) Select the cell or range of cells to be aligned.

(ii) Click the relevant horizontal and vertical alignment buttons from the Alignment group under the Home tab.

Cell Orientation

Cell content can be orientated to be read vertically or at an angle. This can be combined with features like merge cells and cell alignment to create effects as shown below

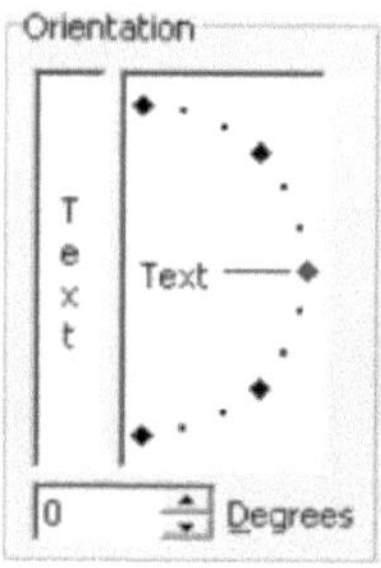

To change the orientation of the cell content, do the following

(i) Select the cell holding the text that you want to orientate.

(ii) Click the Orientation button in the Alignment group, under Home tab.

(iii) Select the desired orientation option from the list which appears.

You can also orientate cell content using the Alignment tab of the Format Cells dialog box that can be opened by clicking on the small arrow in the right corner of the Alignment group, under the Home tab. To orientate cell content, either click and drag the red diamond to the required position or enter the intended degrees in the Degrees field.

Merge Cells

Cells content can be merged and centered across multiple columns or rows making one large cell. To merge and center cell content, do the following

(i) Select the range of cells to be merged and centered.

(ii) Click the Merge & Center option in the Alignment group, under the Home tab.

Note *You should leave a gap between cells that have been merged and other spreadsheet content, as merging cells break up a spreadsheet's structure potentially causing problems with other Excel features.*

Wrap Text

If cell content becomes too large for the column or the row, you can increase the row height or column width, i.e. to wrap the text, do the following

(i) Select the cell or range of cells.

(ii) Click the Wrap Text button in the Alignment group, under the Home tab.

Note *You can also wrap text while entering data into the cell by pressing Alt + Enter.*

Formatting Numbers

Changing the appearance of numbers comes under number formatting. For formatting numbers, do the following

(i) Select the cell or range of cells that you want to format.

(ii) Locate the Number group, under the Home tab.

(iii) Click on the down-facing arrow next to the Number Format button.

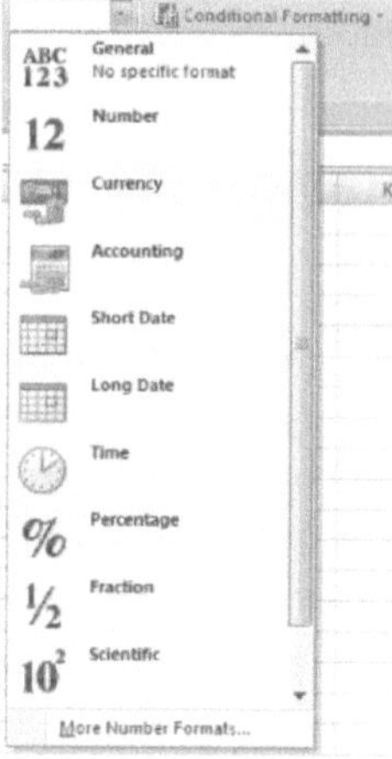

(iv) From the list that will appear, select the number format which you want to apply to the cell or range of cells you selected (e.g. Accounting).

Inserting/Deleting Cells, Rows and Columns

As we already know that an Excel worksheet is always in grid format, i.e. in tabular format. Still it allows you to insertion and deletion of cells, rows and columns when required.

Inserting Cell/Cells

For inserting one or more cells in your worksheet, do the following

(i) Select the cell or range of cells where you want the new blank cell/cells to appear.

(ii) Locate the Cells group under the Home tab.

(iii) Click on the down-facing arrow below the Insert button.

(iv) From the list that appears, select Insert Cells.

(v) From the Insert dialog box that appears, select the desired option.

(vi) Click OK button.

Deleting Cell/Cells

For deleting one or more cells from your worksheet, do the following

(i) Select as many number of cells as you want to delete from your worksheet.

(ii) Locate the Cells group under the Home tab.

(iii) Click on the down-facing arrow below the Delete button.

(iv) From the list that appears, select Delete Cells.

(v) From the Delete dialog box that appears, select the desired option.

(vi) Click OK button.

Inserting Rows/Columns

Before inserting rows/columns in a worksheet, you need to select that row/column above/left where you want to insert the new row/column. For inserting one or more rows/columns in your worksheet, do the following

(i) Select as many numbers of rows/columns, you want to insert in your worksheet.

(ii) Locate the Cells group under the Home tab.

(iii) Click on the down-facing arrow below the Insert button.

(iv) From the list that appears, select Insert Sheet Rows/Columns.

Deleting Rows/Columns

For deleting one or more rows/columns from your worksheet, do the following

(i) Select as many numbers of rows/columns, you want to delete from your worksheet.

(ii) Locate the Cells group under the Home tab.

(iii) Click on the down-facing arrow below the Delete button.

(iv) From the list that appears, select Delete Sheet Rows/Columns.

Working with Formulas and Functions

The biggest advantage of spreadsheet package is that it allows Mathematical calculations and makes them easier by means of formulas.

A formula is a combination of values, operators (+, −, /, *) and cell addresses as operands that perform calculation on the values contained in the cell addresses.

Entering Formula in a Cell

Any formula in Excel starts with an = (equal) sign. It means, if you do not specify = (equal) sign before a formula, either knowingly or accidentally, Excel will treat that as an ordinary text and will not perform any calculation on the contents of that cell. Let us take an example for illustrating the concept of entering a formula in a cell.

Student Name	Mathematics	Science	English	Computer	Total Mark	Percentage
Rahul	70	67	45	91		
Ravi	85	87	88	89		
Avantika	90	67	67	90		
Sapna	60	56	89	98		

The above data must be very much familiar to you as it is a simple table representing partial data of students.

Now, what you want is to calculate the total marks of individual student in column 'G' and also want to calculate percentage of each student in column 'H'.

We can write formula in cell G5 to calculate sum of data values from cells C5 to F5 in order to calculate total marks of student named Rahul. So, in cell G5 we will write like = C5 + D5 + E5 + F5 and press Enter.

As soon as you press Enter, the sum of values from cell C5 to cell F5 will be displayed in cell G5. Similarly, we can calculate the total marks of other students as well.

For calculating the percentage of student Rahul, we can write = G5*100/400 in cell H5 and press Enter. Similarly, we can calculate percentage of other students as well.

Using Operators in Formulae

The calculation that is done by a formula is defined by the operators it contains. To perform basic Mathematical operations such as addition, subtraction, multiplication or division, Excel supports following operators, which are inserted in the formulae.

Arithmetic Operators	Meaning
+ (plus sign)	Addition
− (minus sign)	Subtraction/Negation
* (asterisk)	Multiplication
/ (forward slash)	Division

Cell Referencing

In Excel, cell is referenced by a combination of row number and column letter. Cell referencing is a method by which a cell or series of cells in a formula is referred. Referencing a cell is beneficial in formulas because it allows your formulas to update automatically, if the value in a particular cell changes and can also update formulas as cells are copied or moved.

Three types of cell referencing are as follows

1. Relative Cell Referencing

When we want to copy a formula from one cell to another cell and also, we want to modify the cell references used in the formula according to the new cell, then it is called relative cell referencing. Consider the following example for understanding this concept.

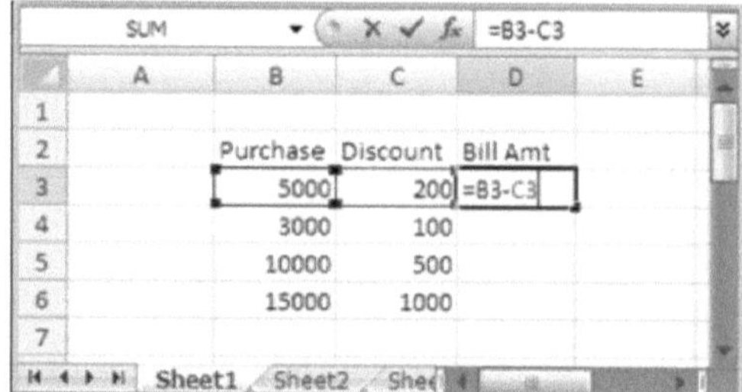

In the given screenshot, for calculating Bill Amt, we have entered formula (= B3 – C3) in cell D3. Now, in case of relative cell referencing, if we will copy this formula in any other cell, the references used in formula B3 and C3 will change accordingly. Let us copy this formula in cell D4. The formula will automatically become (= B4 – C4) in cell D4. Similarly, in cell D5 and D6 you can copy formula using relative referencing.

2. Absolute Cell Referencing

When we want to copy a formula from one cell to another cell, but we do not want to modify the cell references used in the formula according to the new cell, then it is called absolute cell referencing. For making the reference of a cell absolute, we need to use '$' (dollar) sign before row number and column letter. Consider the following example for understanding this concept.

In the above example in cell D3, we have written formula = B3 - C3. Now, when we will copy this formula in cell D4, it will be copied as it is, without any change.

3. Mixed Cell Referencing

When we use '$' sign either before row number or before column letter, then it is called mixed cell referencing. In other words, mixed referencing is a combination of both relative and absolute referencing. Consider the following example for understanding this concept.

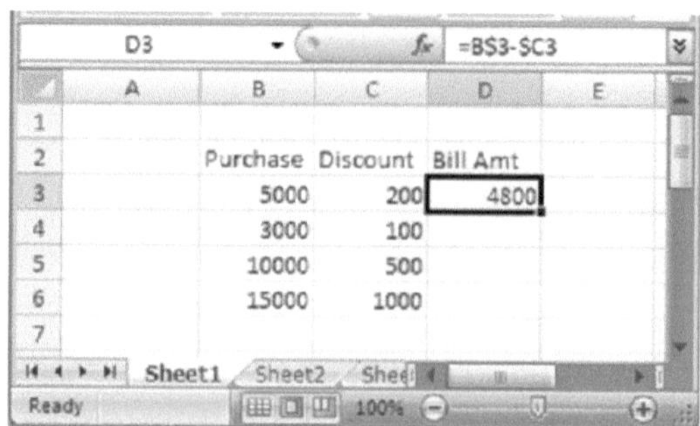

In the above example in cell D3, we have written formula =B$3 - $C3. Now, when we will copy this formula in cell D4, it will be copied as = B$3 - $C4 because of mixed referencing.

Using Functions

Predefined formulas in MS-Excel are called functions. Functions perform calculations on the values provided to them as arguments. Two important parts of any function are arguments and structure.

(i) **Arguments** refer to the values or cell references passed to a function. These are always written within parentheses and can be numbers, text, Boolean values (True or False), constants, functions or formulas.

(ii) **Structure** of function means the way, we write a function in a cell. It starts with function name followed by opening parentheses, then comes comma separated by argument list and finally closing parentheses. In case of formula, start it with = (equal) sign.

Some commonly used functions in MS-Excel are as follows

1. SUM Function

This function, as clear from name, is used to add all the values provided as argument and to display the result in the cell containing function.

Argument Type All Numbers

Return Type Number

Syntax = SUM (number1, number2, ...)

e.g. if you want to display the sum of values of cells A1, A2, A5 and A6 in cell A9, then you need to simply type = SUM(A1,A2,A5,A6) in cell A9 and press Enter. The sum will be displayed in cell A9. If you want to add a values of range, then provide that range in SUM function as an argument. e.g. if you want to add values from A1 to A5, then write like =SUM(A1:A5).

2. AVERAGE Function

This function calculates the average of all the values provided as argument to this function.

Argument Type All Numbers

Return Type Number

Syntax = AVERAGE (number1, number2, ...)

e.g. to calculate the average of the values of range starting from A1 to A5 in cell B9, you need to write = AVERAGE(A1:A5) in cell B9.

3. COUNT Function

This function counts the number of cells that contain numbers and numbers within the list of arguments.

Argument Type Any Type

Return Type Number

Syntax = COUNT (value1, value2, ...)

e.g. if the values contained in cells A1, A2, A3 and A4 are 5, 7, TRUE and 10 respectively, then=COUNT(A1:A4) will return 3.

4. COUNTA Function

This function is similar to the COUNT ( ) function. The only difference is that the COUNTA ( ) function also calculates the text entries even when the entries contain an empty string of length 0(zero), i.e. " ' ", but empty cells are ignored. The COUNTA( ) function counts the total number of values in the list of arguments.

Argument Type Any Type

Return Type Number

Syntax = COUNTA (value1, value2, ...)

e.g. if the value contained in cells A1, A2, A3 and A4 are 5, 7, TRUE and 10 respectively then = COUNTA (A1 : A4) will return 4.

5. MAX Function

This function is used to return maximum value from a list of arguments.

Argument Type All Numbers

Return Type Number

Syntax = MAX(number1, number2, ...)

e.g. if the values contained in cells A1, A2, A3 and A4 are 5, 7, 2 and 10 respectively then = MAX(A1:A4) will return 10.

6. MIN Function

This function is used to return minimum value from a list of arguments.

Argument Type All Numbers

Return Type Number

Syntax = MIN(number1, number2,.....)

e.g. if the values contained in cells A1, A2, A3 and A4 are 5, 7, 2 and 10 respectively then = MIN(A1:A4) will return 2.

7. IF Function

This function is used to compare two values as per some predefined condition and returns a value from them accordingly.

Syntax   = IF(logical_test,
            value_if_true,[value_if_false])

where,

- **logical_test** is required, any value or expression that can be evaluated to TRUE or FALSE. e.g. A10== 100 is a logical expression; if the value in cell A10 is equal to 100, the expression evaluates to TRUE. Otherwise, the expression evaluates to FALSE.

- **value_if_true** is required, the value that you want to be returned, if the logical_test argument evaluates to TRUE. e.g. if the value of the argument is the text string 'Within budget' and the logical_test argument evaluates to TRUE, the IF function returns the text 'Within budget'.

  If logical_test evaluates to TRUE and the value_if_true argument is omitted (that is, there is only a comma following the logical_test argument), the IF function returns 0 (zero). To display the word TRUE, use the logical value TRUE for the value_if_true argument.

- **value_if_false** is optional. The value that you want to be returned, if the logical_test argument evaluates to FALSE. e.g. if the value of this argument is the text string 'Over budget' and the logical_test evaluates to FALSE, the IF function returns the text 'Over budget'. If logical_test evaluates to FALSE and the value_if_false argument is omitted, (that is, there is no comma following the value_if_true argument) the IF function returns the logical value FALSE.

- If logical_test evaluates to FALSE and the value of the value_if_false argument is blank (that is, there is only a comma following the value_if_true argument), the IF function returns the value 0 (zero). e.g. = IF(A10 = 100, 100, "Too small") will return 100, if cell A10 stores value 100 otherwise, it will return string "Too small".

Working with Charts

A chart is a tool that is used in Excel for representing data graphically. Charts allow anyone to more easily see the meaning behind the numbers in the spreadsheet and to make showing comparisons and trends much easier. It is one of the most impressive features of MS-Excel. Endless variations are available, allowing you to produce a chart, edit and format it, include titles and many more.

Types of Chart

Excel provides you different types of charts that suit your purpose.

Based on the type of data, you can create a chart. You can also cange the chart type later.

Excel offers the following major chart types

  (i) Column chart   (ii) Line chart

 (iii) Pie chart   (iv) Bar chart

(v) Area chart   (vi) XY (Scatter) chart
(vii) Stock chart   (viii) Surface chart
(ix) Doughnut chart   (x) Bubble chart
(xi) Radar chart   (xii) Combo chart

The most useful types of chart and their applications are as follows

(i) Line Charts

These types of chart can be 2 or 3-dimensional. Line charts are used to compare trends over time. There are similarities with area charts but line charts tend to emphasise the rate of change rather than volume of change over time. 3-D lines appear as 'ribbons' which can be easier to see on the chart.

(ii) Pie Charts

These types of chart can be 2 or 3-dimensional. They are used to compare the size of the parts with the whole. Only one data series can be plotted, making up 100%. Pie charts within their own window can be made to 'explode' by dragging or more pieces of pie away from the centre.

(iii) Bar Charts

These types of chart can be 2 or 3-dimensional. They are used to show individual figures at a specific time or to compare different items. Categories are listed vertically, so that bars appear on the horizontal, thus there is less emphasis on time flow. Bars extending to the right represent positive values while those extending left represent negative values.

(iv) Area Charts

These types of chart can be 2 or 3-dimensional. They are used to compare the changes in volume of a data series over time, emphasising the amount of change rather than the rate of change. Area charts show clearly, how individual data series contribute to make up the whole volume of information represented in the graph.

(v) XY (Scatter) Charts

These types of chart are used to compare two different numeric data series and can be useful in determining whether one set of figures might be dependent on the other. They are also useful, if the data on the X-axis represents uneven intervals of time or increments of measurement.

Components of Chart

Various components or parts of chart are as follows

(i) **X-axis** Refers to a horizontal axis, which is also known as category axis.
(ii) **Y-axis** Refers to a vertical axis, which is also known as value axis.
(iii) **X-axis title** conveys the full details of the X-axis values.

(iv) **Y-axis title** conveys the full details of the Y-axis values.
(v) **Data series** Refers to a set of data that you want to display in a chart.
(vi) **Chart area** Refers to the total space that is enclosed by a chart.
(vii) **Plot area** Refers to the main region of the chart in which your data is plotted.
(viii) **Chart title** Denotes the type of data plotted in a chart.
(ix) **Legend** In a chart showing different data series, a unique color or pattern is assigned to each data series. This unique color of pattern is known as a legend.
(x) **Gridlines** These are the horizontal and vertical lines within the plot area in a chart.
(xi) **Data label** Provides additional information about a value in the chart, that is coming from a worksheet cell.

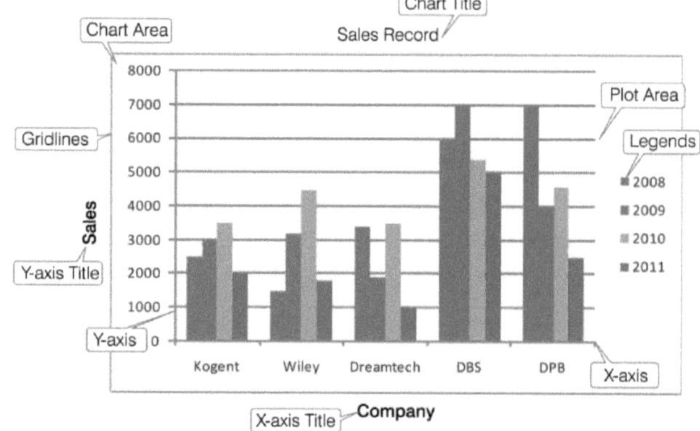

The chart shown in the above figure is based on the worksheet shown below

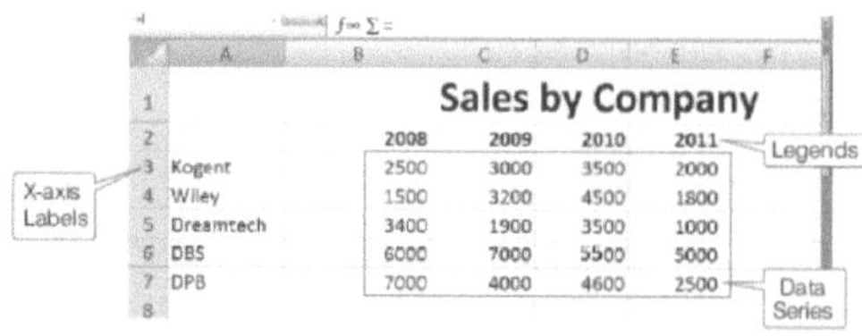

A Sales by Company worksheet

Creating a Chart

Here is a worksheet that shows the marks of students in a class Subject wise. To create a chart, do the following

(i) Select the data that you want to show, including the column titles and the row labels.
(ii) Then click the Insert tab and in the Charts group, click the Column button. You could select another chart type, but column charts are commonly used to compare items.

(iii) After you click Column button you'll see a number of column chart types to choose from. Click Clustered Column which is the first column chart in the 2-D Column list.

A ScreenTip displays the chart type name, when you rest the pointer over any chart type. The ScreenTip also provides a description of the chart type and gives you information about that, when to use each one.

Printing a Worksheet/ Workbook

While working on a worksheet, sometimes you may need to print the entire or partial worksheets, in order to obtain a hardcopy of the work that you have done so far.

For printing partial or entire worksheet, do the following

(i) Do one of the following

To print a partial worksheet, click the worksheet and then select the range of data that you want to print.

or

To print the entire worksheet, click the worksheet to activate it.

or

To print a workbook, click any of its worksheets.

(ii) Click File tab and then click Print. Alternatively, you can also press Ctrl +P on your keyboard.

(iii) Enter the desired number of copies to be printed in the box named Copies under print section.

(iv) Click OK button to confirm.

Chapter Practice

Objective Questions

• Multiple Choice Questions

1. A worksheet is a
(a) collection of workbooks
(b) processing software
(c) combination of rows and columns
(d) None of the above

Ans. (*c*) A worksheet is a combination of rows and columns.

2. By default, a workbook in Excel contains how many worksheets?
(a) 16   (b) 1 or 3   (c) 15   (d) 256

Ans. (*b*) 1 or 3 worksheets are contained by a workbook in Excel. It depends on the version of Excel.

3. .... shortcut keys used to copy a range of data.
(a) Ctrl+V   (b) Ctrl + A   (c) Ctrl + C   (d) Ctrl + X

Ans. (*c*) Ctrl + C shortcut key is used to copy a range of data.

4. The simplest way to move data from one location to another in Excel is
(a) Quick Access toolbar
(b) Using Cut and Paste
(c) By the drag and drop method
(d) Both (b) and (c)

Ans. (*d*) We can move data from one location to another using cut and paste, and also drag and drop method.

5. Arun is a school head and preparing the list of students with their roll no of class IX. Later on, he remembers that he forgot to add the some students' roll no in the mid of the list. Now, what feature of Excel will help him to add the roll no in the mid of the list?
(a) Insert Row
(b) Insert Column
(c) Insert Cell
(d) Delete Row

Ans. (*a*) Arun can add roll numbers of remaining students in between the sheet by using – Insert Row option.

6. Data represented in a worksheet can be easily understood by
(a) Database
(b) Letter
(c) Chart
(d) Symbol

Ans. (*c*) Chart in MS-Excel is used to present data in very visible and predictable way.

7. Cell address A3 in a formula means it is a
(a) Mixed cell reference
(b) Absolute cell reference
(c) Relative cell reference
(d) None of these

Ans. (*c*) When the cell number is based upon the position relative to the cell containing the formula called as relative cell addressing or referencing.

8. Cell address B5 in a formula means
(a) Mixed reference
(b) Absolute reference
(c) Relative reference
(d) None of these

Ans. (*b*) $ sign in a formula need to add before row number and column letter for absolute referencing. e.g. B5.

9. A cell range starting from first row, first column to fourth row and fifth column can be represented as
(a) [A1 : E4]
(b) [A0 : E3]
(c) [E4 : A1]
(d) [E3 : A0]

Ans. (*a*) [A1:E4] because row count starts from 1 and column count starts from A and first we write the starting cell address.

10. Misha wants to store data of her monthly expenditure for a period of two years and also wants to perform some calculation and analysis. Which Microsoft application, will you suggest Misha should use for this purpose and why?
(a) Word
(b) Excel
(c) PowerPoint
(d) Access

Ans. (*b*) Excel or Microsoft Excel should be used because it cannot only be used for storing data, but also be used to perform calculations and analysis of the data.

11. A cell range always has the .... symbol between the cell references.

(a) ;(semicolon) (b) .(full stop)
(c) ,(comma) (d) :(colon)

Ans. (d) A cell range always has the : (colon) symbol between the address of ranges.

12. If cell range A1 : A5 contains the numbers 20, 16, 5, 35 and 7, then = AVERAGE(A1:A5, 50) will display

(a) 22.167 (b) 27.167
(c) 10 (d) 40

Ans. (a) It calculates average of numbers from range A1 to A5 and also 50. So, it will consider 6 numbers.

It finds the average of 20, 16, 5, 35, 7 and 50 which will be 22.167.

13. The another name for the XY chart is

(a) Column chart (b) Net chart
(c) Bar chart (d) Scatter chart

Ans. (d) XY chart is also called as Scatter chart.

14. The sample of an Excel worksheet on the screen can be seen by

(a) Print preview (b) Print
(c) Review (d) None of these

Ans. (a) Print preview enables you to view the sample of worksheet before printing it on a paper.

15. You have used a spreadsheet to calculate the average marks of a class in Mathematics. Which input is essential to find the average marks?

(a) Marks of each student of class in Science.
(b) Marks of each student of class in Mathematics.
(c) Average marks in Mathematics of each student of class.
(d) Names and roll numbers of each student of class.

Ans. (b) Marks of each student of class in Mathematics will be required for calculating average marks of Mathematics.

• Case Based MCQs

Direction *Read the case and answer the following questions.*

16. The teacher has maintained a record of each student in her class in the form of an excel sheet. Each record has Rollno, Name and Marks of the students.

	A	B	C	D
1	Rollno	Name	Marks	
2	1	Amit	50	
3	2	Mradul	23	
4	3	Arun	24	
5	4	Sonali	56	
6	5	Kishan	65	
7	6	Mona	58	
8				

(i) Write formula to find the sum of all marks in a class.

(a) = AVERAGE (C2:C7) (b) = SUM(C2-C7)
(c) = SUM(C2:C7) (d) = SUM(C)

(ii) Write formula to find maximum marks in the class.

(a) = MAX(C2-C7) (b) = MAX(C2:C7)
(c) = MAX(C2;C7) (d) = MAXI(C2:C7)

(iii) Find the total students in the class.

(a) COUNT(A1-A7) (b) COUNT(A2;A7)
(c) COUNT(A2:A7) (d) COUNT(A1;A7)

(iv) What is cell range of second record?

(a) A3-C3 (b) A3:C3 (c) A2-C2 (d) A2:C2

(v) Copy record 3 i.e. row 3 using shortcut keys

(a) Select A4 to C4 for copy use Ctrl+C
(b) Select Whole row and for copy use Ctrl+V
(c) Select A4 to C4 for copy use Ctrl+X
(d) Select A4 to C4 for copy use Ctrl+L

Ans. (i) (c) For finding the sum of all marks the cells C2 to C7 will be used in SUM( ) function as = SUM (C2 : C7).

(ii) (b) For finding the maximum marks in the class the cells C2 to C7 will be used in MAX() function as = MAX (C2 : C7).

(iii) (c) For finding the total students in the class, the cells A2 to A7 will be used in COUNT() function as = COUNT (A2 : A7).

(iv) (b) The second record is started from cell A3 and ends with C3.

(v) (a) Shortcut keys for copy is Ctrl+C and 3rd record i.e. row 3 is A4 to C4.

PART 2

Subjective Questions

• Short Answer Type Questions

1. Write down the significance of electronic spreadsheets.

Ans. Using electronic spreadsheets, large volume of data can be stored in worksheets. Worksheets can be managed, edited, viewed, retrieved and printed easily in desired format. Electronic spreadsheets support charts, which represent data graphically.

2. Is it possible to remove a worksheet? State the process of doing it.

Ans. Yes, it is possible to remove a worksheet. To remove a worksheet, right-click on the Sheets tab of the sheet that you want to delete and choose Delete from pop-up menu, or choose Delete Sheet from the pop-up menu of Delete option on Cells group under Home tab.

3. What do you mean by formula?

Ans. Formula plays a major role in spreadsheet making. A formula is a combination of values, operators and cell addresses as operands that perform calculation on the values contained in the addresses.

4. What is the use of the COUNT( ) function in Excel?

Ans. COUNT( ) function can be used to total the number of cells in a selected range. The COUNT( ) function will add up the number of cells in a selected range that contains numbers.

5. Sana has entered 49+30 in a cell. The worksheet is not displaying 79 in the cell. Instead, 49+30 is getting displayed. Help Sana in rectifying the problem.

Ans. In Excel, every formula must start with an = (equal) sign. Since, Sana has not put = sign before 49+30, thus she is not able to see the desired result will be displayed if she will use = (49 + 30) formula.

6. Suggest the appropriate function for the following situations:

(i) Selecting the maximum value out of a range A1 to B20.

(ii) Calculating average of marks entered in cells E5, F5, G5, H5 and I5.

(iii) Determining whether the student has passed (if scored >= 40) or not from the marks stored in cell J10.

Ans. (i) = MAX(A1 : B20)　　(ii) = AVERAGE(E5: I5)

(iii) =IF(J10 >= 40, "Pass", "Fail")

7. For what purpose pie charts are useful?

Ans. Pie charts are useful for the following purposes

(i) They convey approximate propositional relationship at a point in time.

(ii) They compare part of a whole at a given point in time.

(iii) Exploded portion of a pie chart emphasise a small proportion of parts.

8. In a worksheet, cell K12 has a value. A formula is to be entered in cell K15, such that if the value in cell K12 is more than 300, the value in cell K15 would be 1.33 times the value of cell K12. Otherwise, the value in cell K15 would be 1.5 times the value of cell K12. Explain the formula that you use to achieve this.

Ans. In cell K15, enter the conditional statement = IF (K12 > 300, K12 *1.33, K12 * 1.5). Here, IF condition checks the value at K12, i.e. if it is greater than 300, then calculate 1.33 of K12, otherwise 1.5 of K12.

9. What do you mean by relative referencing?

Ans. In MS-Excel, relative reference refers to the cell referencing technique. In relative referencing, the address of the cells is specified in a way that when the formula is copied to a new cell, the corresponding cell address changes with reference to the new cell address. e.g. = A1+A2

10. How many ways are there for adding a new worksheet in an Excel workbook?

Ans. There are two methods of adding a new worksheet in an Excel workbook, which are as follows

(i) Insert worksheet tab at the bottom.

(ii) Insert button on Cells group under Home tab.

11. Differentiate between the COUNT( ) and COUNTA( ) functions of Excel.

Ans. (i) The COUNT( ) function is generally used to count a range of cells containing numbers or dates excluding blanks. On other hand, COUNTA( ) function will count everything numbers, dates, text or a range containing a mixture of these items, but does not count blank cells.

(ii) COUNT( ) function does not count logical values (TRUE and FALSE), but COUNTA( ) function counts these values.

● Long Answer Type Questions

12. Explain the concept of cell referencing along with its various types.

Ans. Excel supports three types of cell referencing, which are as follows

(i) **Relative** Every relative cell reference in formula automatically changes when the formula is copied down a column or across a row. As the example illustrated here shows, when the formula is entered (= B4 -C4) in cell D4 and copied in D5, then it will change into (= B5 -C5) related to cell.

(ii) **Absolute** This cell reference is fixed. Absolute references do not change if you copy a formula from one cell to another. Absolute references have dollar sign ($) like S9.

e.g. when the formula =C4*D9 is copied from row, the absolute cell reference remains as D9.

(iii) **Mixed** This cell reference has either an absolute column and a relative row or an absolute row and a relative column. e.g. $A1 is an absolute reference to column A and a relative reference to row 1. As a mixed reference is copied from one cell to another, the absolute reference stays the same but the relative reference changes.

13. Explain any five functions that can be used in a worksheet.

Ans. (i) **SUM()** This function is used to add all values of the cells selected as a range.

For example, = SUM (A2:A7) will add values of all the cells from A2 to A7.

(ii) **COUNT()** This function is used to count the number of values in the range of the cells. This function is very useful if anyone wish to count the number of entries in any row or column.

For example, = COUNT(A2:A7)

(iii) **MIN()** This function is used to find the minimum value from the selected range of cells.

For example, = MIN(A2:C5)

(iv) **MAX()** This function is used to find the maximum value from the selected range of cells.

For example, = MAX(A2:C5)

(v) **AVERAGE()** This function is used to find average of all values of the cells selected as a range.

For example, = AVERAGE (A2:A7)

14. Write down the name and purpose of any four components of a chart.

Ans. There are various components of a chart

(i) **X-axis** called as horizontal axis of a chart, which is also known as category axis.

(ii) **Y-axis** called as a vertical axis, which is also known as value axis.

(iii) **Data series** refers to a set of data that you want to display in a chart.

(iv) **Chart area** refers to the total space that is enclosed by a chart.

15. Explain any four types of charts available in Excel.

Ans. The various types of charts in Excel are as follows

(i) **Line Chart** Data that is arranged in columns or rows on a worksheet can be plotted in a line chart. Line charts can display continuous data over time, set against a common scale and are therefore ideal for showing trends in data at equal intervals. In a line chart, category data is distributed evenly along the horizontal axis and all value data is distributed evenly along the vertical axis.

(ii) **Pie Chart** Data that is arranged in one column or row only on a worksheet can be plotted in a pie chart. Pie charts show the size of items in one data series, proportional to the sum of the items. The data points in a pie chart are displayed as a percentage of the whole pie.

(iii) **Scatter Chart** Data that is arranged in columns and rows on a worksheet can be plotted in an XY (scatter)

chart. Scatter charts show the relationships among the numeric values in several data series, or plots two groups of numbers as one series of XY coordinates.

(iv) **Bar Chart** Data that is arranged in columns or rows on a worksheet can be plotted in a bar chart. Bar charts illustrate comparisons among individual items.

16. How are charts created in Excel? Write the steps.

Ans. To create a chart, we require to perform following steps- Lets take example we have following worksheet

Step 1 First of all select the data that is required to present in chart, including the column titles and the row labels.

Step 2 Then click on Insert tab and in the Charts group, there are various chart types are there lets we wish to draw a column chart - select the Column chart button.

Step 3 After selection of chart type, you will find various charts under that, click Clustered Column, the first column chart in the 2-D Column list.

17. What is the differences between a workbook and a worksheet?

Ans. Differences between a workbook and a worksheet are as follows

Workbook	Worksheet
The workbook is just a file or a book.	The worksheet is a single-page spreadsheet.
Adding a workbook to another workbook is not an easy task.	It is easy to add multiple worksheets to a workbook.
A workbook is the general form of data.	The worksheet is specific for a set of data.
It is used to work in a professional environment.	Worksheets are most preferred in an educational or learning environment.
Data manipulation is not possible with a workbook.	Data manipulation and analysis is only possible with worksheets.
Many worksheets can be used at the same time in a workbook.	Using a separate worksheet for different tasks can be complicated or become problematic.

Chapter Test

Multiple Choice Questions

1. In MS-Excel, which symbol is used to start formula?

(a) : (b) $ (c) = (d) ( )

2. Cell address $A4 in a formula means it is a

(a) Mixed cell reference (b) Absolute cell reference
(c) Relative cell reference (d) All of these

3. The keyboard shortcut keys to Copy and Paste are

(a) Ctrl + C and Ctrl+V (b) Ctrl + V and Ctrl+C
(c) Ctrl + X and Ctrl+V (d) Ctrl + C and Ctrl+X

4. When you cut or copy text the selected range gets surrounded by .... border.

(a) Fixed (b) Moving (c) Line (d) None of these

5. Which of the following chart can be used to generate the performance of football team year wise?

(a) Bar (b) Area (c) Pie (d) Scatterplot

6. Bar chart can be used for ....

(a) Present Scientific data (b) Compare groups of data
(c) Show parts of a whole (d) Show activity of an item over a period of time.

7. What do you understand by formatting?

(a) Working in empty worksheet (b) Deleting all items from worksheet
(c) Arranging data in worksheet (d) Delete the worksheet

8. To format size of text in a worksheet, which group will you select from the Home tab?

(a) Format (b) Font (c) Number (d) Alignment

Short Answer Type Questions

9. Charts prove to be a beneficial feature of MS-Excel. How? Name some different types of charts are used in MS-Excel.

10. What is the significance of electronic spreadsheets?

11. What are different types of views available in MS-Excel?

Long Answer Type Questions

12. A company keeps stationery stock of various stationeries in its shop. The proprietor wants to maintain a stock value and reorder level for following items as given in a spreadsheet. Write formulas for the operations (i) to (iii) and answer the questions (iv) and (v) based on the spreadsheet given below along with the relevant cell address:

	A	B	C	D	E	F	G	H
	Item Code	Item Name	Minimum Stock Quantity	Quantity in Stock	Rate	Stock Value	Quantity to Order (Unit)	Order Value
1								
2	101	P. Holder	200	500	35			
3	123	Whitner	450	150	25			
4	113	Steppler Pin	250	450	5			
5	156	Paper cutter	300	600	10			

(i) To calculate the Stock Value as product of 'Quantity in Stock' and 'Rate' for each item present in the spreadsheet.

(ii) To calculate the 'Quantity to Order' as 'Minimum Stock Quantity'-'Quantity in Stock' for each item.

(iii) To calculate the 'Order Value' as product of 'Quantity to Order' and 'Rate' for the items if 'Quantity to Order'>=0, else assign the value as 0.

(iv) The proprietor wants to graphically represent his stationery stock. Suggest him the most appropriate feature of MS-Excel.

(v) If Quantity in Stock's value changes, will we have to redo all the calculations for that particular column? Explain.

13. What are the advantages, disadvantages of using charts or graphs?

Answers

Multiple Choice Questions

1. (c) *2. (a)* *3. (a)* *4. (b)* *5. (a)* *6. (b)* *7. (c)* *8. (b)*

For Detailed Solutions

Scan the code

Practice Paper 1*
(Solved)

General Instructions

- **Time :** 2 Hours
- **Max. Marks :** 25

1. There are 8 questions in the question paper. All questions are compulsory.
2. Question no. 1 is a Case Based Question, which has five MCQs. Each question carries one mark.
3. Question no. 2-6 are Short Answer Type Questions. Each question carries 2 marks.
4. Question no. 7-8 are Long Answer Type Questions. Each question carries 5 marks.
5. There is no overall choice. However, internal choices have been provided in some questions. Students have to attempt only one of the alternatives in such questions.

As exact Blue-print and Pattern for CBSE Term II exams is not released yet. So the pattern of this paper is designed by the author on the basis of trend of past CBSE Papers. Students are advised not to consider the pattern of this paper as official, it is just for practice purpose.

1. Direction *Read the following passage and answer the questions that follows*

Input Device

The devices through which control signals are sent to a computer are termed as input devices. These devices convert the input data into a digital form that is acceptable by the computer system. Some examples of input devices include keyboard, mouse, scanner, touch screen, etc. Specially designed braille keyboards are also available to help the visually impaired for entering data into a computer. Besides, we can now enter data through voice, for example, we can use Google voice search to search the web where we can input the search string through our voice. Data entered through input device is temporarily stored in the main memory (also called RAM) of the computer system. For permanent storage and future use, the data as well as instructions are stored permanently in additional storage locations called secondary memory.

(i) The input devices are used to send .... signals to the computer.

  (a) input   (b) control   (c) read   (d) temporary

(ii) The computer accepts only .... data which is converted by input devices.

  (a) user   (b) input   (c) control   (d) digital

(iii) Which is not an input device?

  (a) Scanner   (b) Mouse   (c) Pen drive   (d) All of these

(iv) .... is used to store data entered through input device.

  (a) RAM   (b) ROM   (c) main memory   (d) Both (a) and (c)

(v) Which memory is required, if user wish to store data for future access?

  (a) Main memory   (b) RAM

  (c) Hard disk   (d) All of these

2. How LAN is different from WAN?

3. How system software is different from application software?

Or What is the difference between compiler and interpreter?

4. Explain, memory stick and pen drive as a secondary storage device.

5. What do you mean by guided transmission media? Give any two example.

Or What are the shortcut keys of Cut, Copy and Paste?

6. Explain in brief any two views of PowerPoint slides.

Or Differentiate between wired and wireless media used in communication network.

7. Draw a clean block diagram of a computer with all its components. Explain the use of ALU.

Or Write some applications of computers.

8. What is RAM memory? Define the various types of RAM.

Or Write any two similarities and two differences between laser and inkjet printers.

Explanations

1. (i) (*b*) The input devices are used to send control signals to the computer. Input devices convert the input data into a digital form that is acceptable by the computer system.

(ii) (*d*) The input device accepts user data and converts into digital data, which is accepted by computer.

(iii) (*d*) Mention all devices in options are the input device. Scanner used to scan all the images or pictures, mouse is a pointing input device. Pen drive is a secondary storage device which can be used to read data which is stored in it.

(iv) (*d*) The RAM is called as main memory used to store all the data input by input devices.

(v) (*c*) If the user wish to access data in future, then he requires to store it permanently. Hard disk is a secondary storage device, which is used to store data permanently.

2. The differences between LAN and WAN are as follows

Parameter	LAN	WAN
Geographical Area	It can be built-in a building.	It can be across continents.
Cost	Less	High
Distance	Upto 1 km	Unlimited

3. The differences between system software and application software are as follows

System Software	Application Software
System Software maintain the system resources and give the path for application software to run.	Application software is built for specific tasks.
Low level languages are used to write the system software.	High level languages are used to write the application software.
Without system software, system cannot run.	While without application software system always runs.

Or

The differences between compiler and interpreter are as follows

Compiler	Interpreter
Compiler converts the whole source code of high level language in machine code in one go.	Interpreter converts line by line source code in machine code.
Its speed is fast.	Its speed is slow.

4. Memory stick It is a kind of portable card, which is release by Sony Company at the end of 1998. Memory stick is a USB based flash drive. It is used in digital cameras as an external storage to store the data of the camera.

Pen drive It is also called as a flash drive. It is used as a portable secondary storage device. The data can be stored in the pen drive using a USB port of the computer and it can be then carried anywhere.

5. The communication channel which carries signal with a particular direction and guidance called as guided media. Generally, using these media the signals travels through a cables and wires in a particular direction only in a bounded way.

e.g. (i) Co-axial cable   (ii) Fibre optics

Or

Cut – Ctrl + X, Copy – Ctrl + C, Paste- Ctrl +V

6. Normal view This is the main editing view, where you write and design your presentations, i.e. actual screen which is displayed. The view is also known as slide view. A Normal view is the default view size for the screen.

Slide Sorter view It provides a view of slides in thumbnail form. This view makes it easy to sort and organise the sequence of the slides at the time of creating presentation and also, at the time of preparing presentation for printing.

Or

The differences between wired and wireless communication media are as follows

Parameters	Wired Communication Media	Wireless Communication Media
Speed	High speed	Low than wired
Security	High	Low
Distance	Limited	Unlimited
Reliability	High	Low
Cost	High	Low

7.

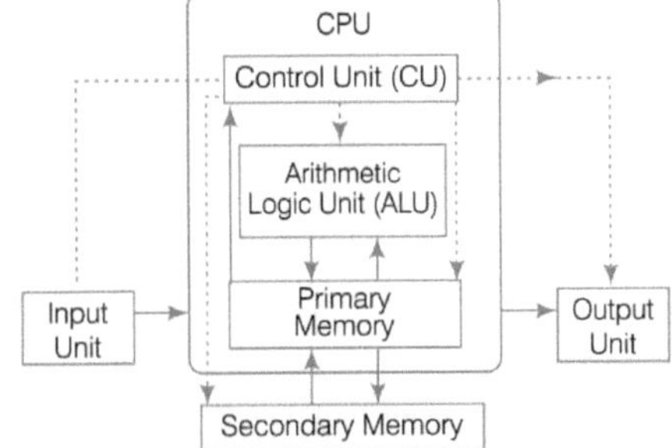

ALU (Arithmetic and Logic Unit) is a part of CPU. The ALU is responsible to perform all the arithmetic and logical operation submitted to the computer by a user. ALUs can perform the following operations

(i) **Arithmetic operations** (addition (+), subtraction (–), multiplication (*) and division (/)).

(ii) **Logical operations** (AND, NOT, OR, XOR).

(iii) **Bit-shifting operations** (shifting or rotating a word by a specified number of bits to the left or right, with or without sign extension).

(iv) **Comparison operations** (=, <, <=, >, >=).

Or

Now-a-days computer is used everywhere in almost every part of our day to day life. Whether it is in home, business, educational institutions, research organizations, medical field, government offices, entertainment, etc.

(i) **Home** Computers are used at homes for several purposes like online bill payment, watching movies or shows at home, home tutoring, social media access, playing games, internet access, etc. They provide communication through electronic mail. They help to avail work from home facility for corporate employees. Computers help the student community to avail online educational support.

(ii) **Medical Field** Computers are used in hospitals to maintain a database of patients' history,

diagnosis, X-rays, live monitoring of patients, etc. Surgeons now-a-days use robotic surgical devices to perform delicate operations and conduct surgeries remotely. Virtual reality technologies are also used for training purposes.

(iii) **Entertainment** Computers help to watch movies online, play games online; act as a virtual entertainer in playing games, listening to music, etc. MIDI instruments greatly help people in the entertainment industry in recording music with artificial instruments. Videos can be fed from computers to full screen televisions. Photo editors are available with fabulous features.

(iv) **Industry** Computers are used to perform several tasks in industries like managing inventory, designing purpose, creating virtual sample products, interior designing, video conferencing, etc. Online marketing has seen a great revolution in its ability to sell various products to inaccessible corners like interior or rural areas. Stock markets have seen phenomenal participation from different levels of people through the use of computers.

8. RAM is called as an internal memory which is used by computer to read and write instructions and data at the time of processing. This memory is often associated with volatile types of memory, which means the data is available only till power is ON, because it requires a continuous flow of electrical current. If current is interrupted, data is lost. It is an integrated circuit that enables you to access the stored data in a random order constantly.

Two main forms of RAM are as follows

(i) **SRAM (Static RAM)** It is a computer memory that requires a constant power flow in order to hold information. It is more expensive which requires more power, therefore it is commonly used in cache and video card memory.

(ii) **DRAM (Dynamic RAM)** It stores information in a cell containing a capacitor and transistor, these cells must be refreshed with electric impulses in few milliseconds. This process allows memory to keep charge which hold the data as long as needed. Also, it is slower than SRAM.

Or

Inkjet	Laser
Similarities	
Non-impact printer	Non-impact printer
Required to refill	Required to refill
Differences	
Less in cost	High in cost
Speed slow	Speed fast
Ink life is very short.	It has a toner and life is quite long.

Practice Paper 2*
(Solved)

1. Direction *Read the following passage and answer the questions that follows*

Software

The computer has two parts-hardware and software. Hardware needs to be operated by a set of instructions. These sets of instructions are referred to as software. It is that component of a computer system, which we cannot touch or view physically. It comprises the instructions and data to be processed using the computer hardware. The computer software and hardware complete any task together. The software comprises a set of instructions which on execution deliver the desired outcome. In other words, each software is written for some computational purpose. Some examples of software include operating systems like Ubuntu or Windows 7/10, Word processing tool like LibreOffice or Microsoft Word, video player like VLC Player, photo editors like GIMP and LibreOffice draw. A document or image stored on the hard disk or pen drive is referred to as a soft copy. Once printed, the document or an image is called a hard copy.

(i) Hardware can work only with ....

  (a) input   (b) control   (c) signals   (d) instructions

(ii) The computer software cannot be .... physically.

  (a) set   (b) touch   (c) control   (d) digital

(iii) Any task of the computer can be completed by .... and .... together.

  (a) input, output   (b) mouse, printer
  (c) hardware, software   (d) All of these

(iv) Which is not an operating system software?

  (a) Windows   (b) DOS   (c) MS-Word   (d) Ubuntu

(v) A document stored on pen drive is called as ....

  (a) soft copy   (b) copy   (c) data   (d) All of these

2. Why formatting is necessary?

Or Why networking is needed?

3. Explain copy, cut and paste operations in any application software such as MS-Excel or MS-PowerPoint.

4. Write any three limitations of internal memory.

Or Write the steps to insert a picture in a slide from computer in PowerPoint.

5. What do you mean by specific purpose application softwares?

6. Differentiate between primary and secondary memory.

Or Write any three basic elements of a slide.

7. Write short note on monitor as an output device.

Or Explain the components of CPU.

8. What are general purpose application software? Why do we use railway reservation system?

Or Define any five parameters of the memory.

Explanations

1.   (i) (*d*) To operate the hardware of a computer it requires some set of instructions to be given.

    (ii) (*b*) The software part of the computer is a non-physical part, which cannot be touch or view.

    (iii) (*c*) Hardware and software are two parts of the computer and any task on the computer can be completed by only these two together.

    (iv) (*c*) Except MS-Word all software comes under the category of OS. MS-Word is a general purpose application software.

    (v) (*a*) Any data in the form of a document stored on secondary storage such as pen drive or hard disk is called soft copy.

2. Formatting is necessary for following reasons

    (i) Formatting makes any document look more presentable and professional.

    (ii) It makes it more interesting and easy to read for the reader.

    (iii) Proper punctuation marks and spelling is preferred for making it look effective.

Or

A computer network is an interconnection of various computers to share software, hardware, resources and data through a communication medium between them. A computer networking is a set of autonomous computers that permits distributed processing of the information and data and increased communication of resources.

3. **Copy** It is an operation through which matter can be copied, matter will be stored in a short memory buffer called as clipborad. When we copy any matter to some other place then the matter will be present at old location as well as new location.

  Cut It is an operation through which matter can be Move, matter will be stored in a short memory buffer called as clipborad. When we cut any matter then the matter will be deleted from old location and will be present in new location. Cut is also called as MOVE.

  Paste It is join operation, which is used either after copy or cut. The paste operation copy back the matter cut or paste by the user in a clipboard to the current location.

4. The internal memory is a memory which is in-built in the CPU. The main limitations are as follows

    (i) Limited in size

    (ii) Volatile (temporary) in nature

    (iii) Cost is high

Or

    (i) Click where you want to insert picture.

    (ii) Select Insert menu and Picture option.

    (iii) Select image file that you want to insert and click on OK.

5. Specific purpose software is a type of software, created to execute one specific task or can be developed as per the requirements of the specific users.

  For example, Hotel Management, Reservation System, Attendance System, Billing System etc.

  These softwares are called as specific purpose application softwares because they target or address a very narrow solution to a problem. It may also be created in house and tailored to the specific needs of a user. The type of software developed to meet particular user specified requirements also falls into this category.

6. The differences between primary memory and secondary memory are as follows

Primary Memory	Secondary Memory
It is temporary.	It is permanent.
It is in-built in CPU.	It is attached externally.
Cost is high.	Cost is less comparatively.

Or

A slide is said to be good, if it conveys the idea in an easy and yet effective manner. The three elements of the slide are as follows

(i) **Title** The heading of a slide is called a title. It represents an idea to the audience about slide contents.

(ii) **Subtitle** The description of the slide data is called a subtitle. It gives more elaborated detail of the central idea of a slide.

(iii) **Text** The entered content by user as bullets on the slide are called text.

7. A monitor also called as a Visual Display Unit (VDU) is an electronic visual device, which is used to display the output. The rectangular area of the monitor, its refresh rate and dot pitch, all directly affect the resolution of the display. Resolution of the monitor refers to the clarity of screen and measured by number of pixels scattered on the screen. The most popular type of monitors in the marks are as follows

(i) **CRT (Cathode Ray Tube)** It works in the same way as a television. It contains an electron gun at the back of the glass tube. This gun fires electrons in a group of phosphor dots, which is coated inside the screen. When electrons strike the phosphor dots, they glow to give the colors.

(ii) **LCD (Liquid Crystal Display)** These screens are used in laptops and notebook sized PCs. A special type of liquid is sandwiched between two plates. It is a thin, flat and light weight screen made up of any number of colors or monochrome pixels arranged in front of a light source.

(iii) **LED (Liquid/Light Emitting Diode)** It is an electronic device that emits light when electrical current is passed through it. It usually produces red light, but now-a-days LEDs can produce RGB (Red, Green and Blue) light and white light also.

Or

CPU is the electronic circuitry of a computer that carries out the actual processing and usually referred as the brain of the computer. It is commonly called processor also. Physically, a CPU can be placed on one or more microchips called integrated circuits (IC). The ICs comprise semiconductor materials.

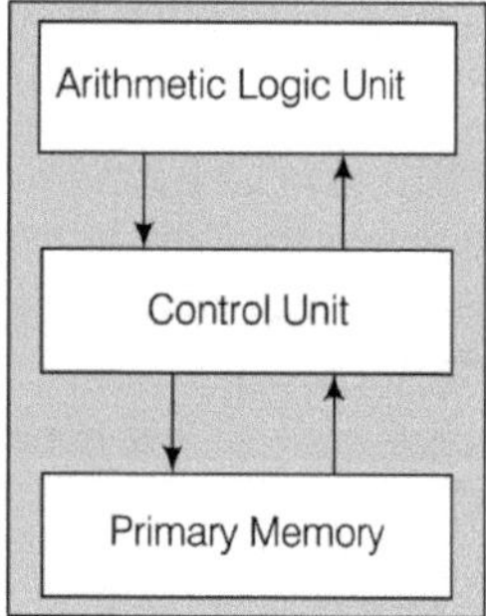

The CPU is given instructions and data through programs. The CPU then fetches the program and data from the memory and performs arithmetic and logic operations as per the given instructions and stores the result back to memory. While processing, the CPU stores the data as well as instructions in its local memory called registers.

Registers are part of the CPU chip and they are limited in size and number. Different registers are used for storing data, instructions or intermediate results. Other than the registers, the CPU has two main components — Arithmetic Logic Unit (ALU) and Control Unit (CU).

ALU performs all the arithmetic and logic operations that need to be done as per the instruction in a program.

CU controls sequential instruction execution, interprets instructions and guides data flow through the computer's memory, ALU and input or output devices. CPU is also popularly known as microprocessor.

8. General purpose application software is a software which is used for any general function. It allows people to do simple computer tasks. General purpose software is sometimes referred to as GPS. e.g. Word Processing Software, Electronic Spreadsheets, Database Management Systems, Desktop Publishing Software, Graphics, Multimedia, Presentation Software etc.

Railway Reservation System It is a computerised system used to store and retrieve information and conduct transactions related to air travel, hotels, car rental or other activities. It is an application software which is commonly seen at railway reservation offices, this software helps the concerned department to automatically check the availability of the seats or berths of any train and on any particular date with an incomparable speed.

Or

The five parameters of the memory are as follows

(i) **Storage capacity** It is represented by size of the memory. The storage capacity of a memory can be measured by number of words or bytes.

(ii) **Access Mode** There are can be three type of accessing modes of the memory sequential, random and direct. These access modes defines how the data stored on different memory locations can be accessed.

(iii) **Access Time** It is a time required by a memory in a particular access mode to read or write a data on a particular memory location.

(iv) **Throughput** It is defined by an amount of information exchanged per unit of time. It is expressed in bits per second.

(v) **Cycle Time** It is a minimum time interval between two successive accesses.

Practice Paper 3*
(Solved)

General Instructions

- **Time :** 2 Hours
- **Max. Marks :** 25

1. There are 8 questions in the question paper. All questions are compulsory.
2. Question no. 1 is a Case Based Question, which has five MCQs. Each question carries one mark.
3. Question no. 2-6 are Short Answer Type Questions. Each question carries 2 marks.
4. Question no. 7-8 are Long Answer Type Questions. Each question carries 5 marks.
5. There is no overall choice. However, internal choices have been provided in some questions. Students have to attempt only one of the alternatives in such questions.

** As exact Blue-print and Pattern for CBSE Term II exams is not released yet. So the pattern of this paper is designed by the author on the basis of trend of past CBSE Papers. Students are advised not to consider the pattern of this paper as official, it is just for practice purpose.*

1. **Direction** *Read the following passage and answer the questions that follows*

   Operating System

   An Operating System (OS) is a system software which can be considered to be a resource manager. It manages all the resources of a computer, i.e. its hardware including CPU, RAM, Disk, Network and other input-output devices. It also controls various application software and device drivers, manages system security and handles access by different users. It is the most important system software. Examples of popular OS are Windows, Linux, Android, Macintosh and so on. The operating system has two primary objectives. The first is to provide services for building and running application programs. When an application program needs to be run, it is the operating system which loads that program into memory and allocates it to the CPU for execution. When multiple application programs need to be run, the operating system decides the order of the execution. The second objective of an operating system is to provide an interface to the user through which the user can interact with the computer. A user interface is a software component which is a part of the operating system and whose job is to take commands or inputs from a user for the operating system to process.

   (i) The another name of resource manager is
   - (a) software
   - (b) operating system
   - (c) processor
   - (d) CPU

   (ii) The resource which cannot be manage by OS is
   - (a) device
   - (b) user
   - (c) process
   - (d) application software

   (iii) The task which cannot be done by OS
   - (a) device management
   - (b) process management
   - (c) error handling
   - (d) All of these

  (iv) Two primary objectives of OS are
- (a) services to application and interface to user
- (b) services to user and interface to applications
- (c) services to devices and interface to users
- (d) None of the above

  (v) The .... is a software component and part of OS.
- (a) main memory
- (b) application
- (c) user interface
- (d) All of these

2. How header and footer are useful?

Or Mr. Vijay is an owner of a super store. Suggest which kind of devices and softwares he need to purchase for following tasks.

  (i) Read the price of an item purchased by a customer.

  (ii) Every day sales status report.

  (iii) Send soft copy of a bill, if some error occur in the printer.

3. The administrative department of a school wants to make a copy of the entire data of the school after each year for the future reference in a soft copy.

  (i) Which type of storage device they can use?

  (ii) What category of software will be required for this purpose?

4. Write any three components of the MS-PowerPoint window.

5. What is equation editor and worksheet in MS-Excel?

Or Differentiate between workbook and worksheet.

6. Define accuracy and diligence as a characteristics of a computer.

Or Write the advantages and disadvantages of ROM.

7. Define the need of computer network.

Or What is the use of ethernet cables? Write the advantages and disadvantages of ethernet cables.

8. What are the different types of slide layouts are there? Explain any one of them.

Or Explain any five types of charts in MS-Excel.

Explanations

1. (i) *(b)* The operating system is also called as a resource manager.

  (ii) *(b)* The OS can manage all the resource of the computer. The user does not comes under the category of computer resource.

  (iii) *(d)* Mention all task can be managed by the OS.

  (iv) *(a)* Two primary objectives of OS are as follows
    (i) Providing services to application programs.
    (ii) Interface to user for interaction with computer.

  (v) *(c)* The user interface is a software component which is a part of OS.

2. Headers and footers are the top and bottom sections of the document respectively. They are separate sections from the main document and are often used to hold footnotes, page numbers, titles and other information. The information in the header or footer is repeated in every header or footer in the document.

e.g. If name of a company which is required to be shown on each page top then should be written in the header.

Or

  (i) Bar code scanner is required to purchase, so that bar codes of the items can be scanner and price can be identified.

  (ii) MS-Excel or Telly softwares will be required to maintain the status of day wise sales.

  (iii) E-mail – such as G-mail or Yahoomail will be required to send the softcopy of the bill to the customer.

3. (i) The school can purchase extra hard disk as a secondary storage device and store all the data in it.

  (ii) The utility system software called as backup software required to be install for taking the backup of all the data of the computer.

4. The three components of the MS-PowerPoint window are as follows
    (i) **Title bar** It contains the name of currently opened file followed by software name.
    (ii) **Ribbon** It is same as Word and Excel, just few tabs are different like Animations, Slide Show etc.
    (iii) **Slide** It appears in the centre of the window. You can create your presentation by adding content to the slides.

5. **Equation editor** It is found below the ribbon menu. Its left side denotes which cell is selected ('A1'), where 'A' a row number and '1' represents column number. It is also called as Cell Address and the right side allows you to input equations or text into the selected cell, called Formula Bar.

    WorkSheet The primary document that you use in Microsoft Excel to store and work with data is a worksheet or sheet. A worksheet is always stored in a workbook. The number of sheets can be increased or decreased as per requirement. Using add button.

Or

Both are used in MS-Excel. The main differences between both are as follows

Workbook	Worksheet
The workbook is a file or a book.	It is single page spreadsheet.
It consists with one or more worksheets.	It consist with row and columns (Matrix kind of structure).

6. **Accuracy** Computer operates with very high degree of accuracy and can do 100% error free calculations. It does not get exhausted to the extent of making mistakes.

    Diligence Unlike human beings, a computer is free from monotony, tiredness, lack of concentration etc. and can do work for hours without creating any errors.

Or

The advantages of ROM are as follows
    (i) Non-volatile in nature.
    (ii) Design can be easily changed or modified.
    (iii) Cheaper and more reliable than RAMs.

The disadvantages of ROM are as follows
    (i) More power consumption.
    (ii) Data is physically encoded in a circuit, so it can only be programmed during fabrication.
    (iii) It cannot be altered.

7. When there are number of computers are connected together with a communication link to share data, information and resources, then it is called as a computer network.

More need of computer network are as follows
    (i) **File and Data Sharing** With networking, files can be shared instantaneously across the network, whether with one user or with hundred users. e.g. employees across departments can collaborate on documents, exchange background material etc.
    (ii) **Resource Sharing** Computer networking also allows the sharing of network resources, such as printers, scanners, dedicated servers, backup systems, input devices and Internet connections. By sharing resources, unique equipment like scanners, printers etc., can be made available to all network users simultaneously without being relocated, eliminating the need for expensive redundancies.
    (iii) **Ease of Administration** Instead of individually upgrading each computer in an organisation, a network administrator can initiate an upgrade from a server and automatically duplicate the upgrade throughout the network. Simultaneously, allowing everyone in the company to maintain uniform software, resources and procedures. It also allows users to communicate using E-mail, newsgroups, video conferencing etc.
    (iv) **Distributed Computing Power** In computer networks, we can distribute tasks across multiple computers throughout the network, by breaking complex problems into hundreds or thousands of smaller operations, which are then parcelled out to individual computers. Each computer in the network performs its operations on its own portion of the larger problem and return its result.

Or

An ethernet cable is one of the most popular form of network cables which are used in wired networks. It is used to build LAN networks. It connects various devices available locally on LAN, such as PCs, Printers, routers and switches, etc. A crossover cable is a special type of ethernet cable specially designed for connecting two computers to each other. By contrast, most ethernet cables are designed to connect one computer to a router or a switch. A single ethernet cable can extend only limited distances due to their electrical transmission characteristics. RJ-45 is the most commonly used Ethernet cable.

Advantages of Ethernet Cable
    (i) It gives fast, secured, reliable transmission across them and external disturbances are very less.
    (ii) You can transfer any large data between two or more PC's which are locally connected through Ethernet.
    (iii) These are robust to noise, thus external disturbances are very less.

Disadvantages of Ethernet Cable

   (i) As the load on Ethernet increases, number of collision increases, therefore efficiency decreases.

   (ii) It offers non-deterministic service, so it is not suitable for real-time application.

   (iii) Higher costs for provisioning in existing building.

8. In MS-PowerPoint there are two types of slide layout are possible- standard and custom. In standard layout, various type of built-in layouts are present while using custom layout user can design a slide as per his requirement.

Standard Layouts The standard, built-in layouts available in Office PowerPoint 2010 are similar to those available in PowerPoint 2003 and earlier versions. When you open a blank presentation in PowerPoint, the default layout called Title Slide (Shown) will appear, but there are other standard layouts that can be applied and used. Other layouts that are present in standard layout are as follows

   (i) Title and Content

   (ii) Section Header

   (iii) Two Content

   (iv) Comparison

   (v) Title Only

   (vi) Blank

   (vii) Content with Caption

   (viii) Picture with Caption

Or

The most useful types of charts used in MS-Excel and their applications are as follows

   (i) **Line Charts** These types of chart can be 2 or 3-dimensional. Line charts are used to compare trends over time. 3-D lines appear as 'ribbons' which can be easier to see on the chart.

   (ii) **Pie Charts** These types of chart can also be 2 or 3-dimensional. They are used to compare the size of the parts with the whole. Only one data series can be plotted, making up 100%.

   (iii) **Bar Charts** These types of chart can also be 2 or 3-dimensional. They are used to show individual figures at a specific time or to compare different items. Categories are listed vertically, so that bars appear on the horizontal, thus there is less emphasis on time flow.

   (iv) **Area Charts** These types of chart can be 2 or 3-dimensional. They are used to compare the changes in volume of a data series over time, emphasising the amount of change rather than the rate of change. Area charts show clearly, how individual data series contribute to make up the whole volume of information represented in the graph.

   (v) **XY Scatter Charts** These types of chart are used to compare two different numeric data series and can be useful in determining whether one set of figures might be dependent on the other. These type of chart also called as scatter chart.

Printed by Libri Plureos GmbH in Hamburg, Germany